# IT's OUR MUSIC TOO
## *The Black Experience*
## *in Classical Music*

# It's Our Music Too
## *The Black Experience in Classical Music*

by
Earl Ofari Hutchinson

MID|DLE
PASS|AGE
PRESS

It's Our Music Too: The Black Experience in Classical Music

Printed in the United States

Published by
Middle Passage Press
5517 Secrest Drive
Los Angeles, California 90043

*Indexed by Barbara Bramwell Hutchinson*
*Designed by Alan Bell*

Publisher's Cataloging-in-Publication
(Provided by Quality Books, Inc.)
Hutchinson, Earl Ofari, author.
It's our music too : the Black experience in classical music /
by Earl Ofari Hutchinson.
pages. cm.
Includes bibliographical references and index.
ISBN 978-0692781876
1. Blacks—Music—History and criticism.
2. Music—History and criticism.
3. Musicians, Black.
4. African American musicians.
5. African Americans—Music—History and criticism.
I. Title.
ML3545.H88    2016
781.68089'96
QBI16-900043

Library of Congress Control Number: 2016915838
Middle Passage Press, Los Angeles, California

# Table of Contents

*On May 18 1803,*

*Ludwig van Beethoven*

*wrote to a patron:*

*"I do not hesitate to recommend to you*

*the bearer, Herr Bridgetower,*

*a very capable virtuoso who has a*

*complete command of his instrument."*

*He referred to George Bridgetower,*

*violin virtuoso supreme and composer,*

*and of African ancestry.*

George Bridgetower

# Introduction

"Noch einmal, mein lieber Bursch!" ("Once more, my dear fellow!"). This is what an excitable, ecstatic, Ludwig van Beethoven shouted across the stage at George Bridgetower. He then burst across the stage to give him a big, bear hug. The occasion was a public performance at the Augarten Theater on May 24, 1803, in Vienna of Beethoven's newly minted *Violin Sonata No. 9 in A Major*. Bridgetower was the object of the master's enthusiastic embrace because he had played the violin part so well during the public concert.

That Beethoven would express his delight with Bridgetower with an animated embrace was really no surprise. Bridgetower had suggested to Beethoven that he compose the sonata. The plan they had worked out earlier was that he would then accompany Beethoven in the playing of it at a public performance. Beethoven was even more enthusiastic about the prospect of their playing together since Bridgetower was widely hailed by Europe's Kings and Queens and wealthy patrons of the arts as one of Europe's finest violin virtuoso performers. The *Sonata in A Major* is often called one of Beethoven's greatest sonatas and among the best in Western classical music.

It was certainly no accident that Bridgetower, the son of a Polish nobleman and West Indian mother, a man of African-ancestry, should be held in such high regard by Beethoven. Or, that he should play a part in the composition of an important classical musical piece. Later, we'll return to Bridgetower to discuss his work before, during and after his appearance with Beethoven.

The Bridgetower-Beethoven collaboration is yet another of the rich and revealing chapters in the often hidden, much ignored, and too frequently marginalized black experience in, and influence on, classical music. There are numerous books which have dissected and re-dissected every possible aspect of classical music—the composers, performers, their compositions, the musical structure, the history, and even the gossip and minutiae about the composers and performers. Yet, there is only a single book, *Blacks in Classical Music* (1978) by singer and music critic Raoul Abdul, published four decades ago, that focuses on the significant part that black composers and performers played in influencing and, in turn, being influenced by classical music. Another book, *Blacks in Classical Music: A Bibliographical Guide to Composers, Performers, and Ensembles (Music Reference Collection)* (1988), is a standard compendium of black classical composers and performers. It is also out of print.

 **Recommended Listening**

Miles Davis, *Sketches of Spain with Joaquin Rodrigo's Concierto de Aranjuez: Adagio*
George Gershwin, *Second Rhapsody*

The reason the influence of blacks on classical music has been ignored or marginalized isn't hard to find. Like many others, I once thought of classical music as a pure, insular, elite European musical form. The even more pronounced perception by many is that it is a stodgy, stuffy, upper-crust music written by a bunch of long dead European white guys. A look around any concert hall on any given night seemingly serves as proof of that. In most cases, one can spot only a handful of persons of color, especially African-Americans, in the audience.

I often watched Robert Lee Watt, an African-American French hornist for more than thirty years with the L.A. Philharmonic Orchestra, play with the orchestra. In his book, *The Black Horn: The Story of Classical French Hornist Robert Lee Watt,* he notes, "In all of my 3-plus decades in the orchestra, out of 3,800 patrons, maybe 20 black folks were present at any given concert. On several occasions, I met some of these uncomfortable black patrons at concert intermissions. They always approached me with great caution, and what annoyed me most about them was that they constantly whispered."

I look at this differently than Watt. The paucity of African-Americans at most classical concerts has absolutely nothing to do with the supposed pure-bred, racially exclusive Eurocentrism of the music that supposedly causes concert halls to resemble a white, elite country club. The true measure of classical music's universal, emotive, and cross-cultural adaptability is its own history. The list of Africans, African-Americans and Afro-European composers, conductors, instrumental performers, and singers is and always has been, rich, varied, and deep. Sadly, the recognition of this history has almost always come in relation to the work of a major European or white American composer.

Two textbook examples of this are two major works by two of classical music's giants. One is the French composer and keyboard virtuoso, Camille Saint-Saens's (1835-1921), *Africa, for Piano and Orchestra, No. 89*, and the other is Czech composer Antonin Dvořák's (1841-1904), the *Symphony No. 9 in E Minor, "From the New World,"* that extensively incorporates Negro Spiritual themes.

 **Recommended Listening**

Dmitri Shostakovich, *Suite for Jazz Orchestra, No. 1*
Camille Saint-Saens, *Africa, for Piano and Orchestra, No. 89*

Classical music artists of African descent began to compose and play not 20, 50, or even 100 years ago. But as early as 500 years ago. Black trumpeter John Blanke served England's Kings Henry VII and VIII as a court musician. A tapestry captures an image of him performing in 1511. Blanke is in the embroidery pictorial because the King, Henry the VIII that is, demanded that there be a pictorial record; so he commissioned what came to be known as the Westminster Roll. The roll actually shows that Blanke was not just another of the many King's court musicians but that he occupied a centerpiece position in the roll. He is depicted twice in the roll.

Blanke certainly knew the value to the court of his musical skills. He had the temerity to demand that Henry pay him what he thought he was worth as a performer. His petition to the king for a pay raise stands as a classic example of how an early classical music performer who played and influenced musical ceremonies and events held by the nobility valued his art. Blanke's petition for a pay increase reads in part:

*"That where as his wage nowe and as yet is not sufficient to mayntaigne and kepe hym to doo your grace lyke service as other your trompeters doo."*

Blanke was a King's court musician, and the music that he and other court musicians played in the sixteenth and seventeen centuries were fanfares, ballads, and song accompaniments. The concerto and symphonic forms were not in the birth stage of musical evolution at that time. This would have to wait until the eighteenth century, and the arrival of Handel,

Vivaldi, Bach, Haydn, Mozart, and the early Beethoven. The evolution of the music of that era also required a framework of understanding of just how the music should be constructed and played.

Ignatius Sancho was one of many who took a stab at laying out a blueprint of his conception of the structure of classical music. Born on a slave ship near West Africa, Sancho was raised in England and feted by the British aristocracy. He began composing in earnest in the 1770s. Fourteen of his pieces, including six minuets, have been recorded and have been made available by the Museum of Richmond as part of their "Trading in Human Lives: The Richmond Connection." In 2007, the noted African-American conductor, and founder of the Chicago Sinfonietta, Paul Freeman performed and recorded electronic instrumental versions of some of Sancho's songs and dances.

However, Sancho made an even more lasting mark by imitating the practice of a number of other classical music heavyweights. He published a series of four collections of his music. Purportedly included in the collection is what a biographer loosely calls, *A Theory of Music* which is dedicated to a British princess. The collection was almost certainly little more than a fragmentary musing about his own music and how it should be regarded and perhaps even played.

A century later, Saint-Saens hit the road every chance he got. He was one of those guys who simply didn't feel right if he wasn't on a boat or a train going somewhere. One of his globe-trotting treks took him to Africa. As soon as he got a glimpse at the sights and lent an ear to the sounds there, he was hooked. In 1891, he tried to capture a bit of the feel and the sense of being in what was then still seen as an exotic, even primal, faraway place in his single movement *Fantasia Africa* (1891) for piano and orchestra. It's not a long piece, but it's especially memorable for his skillful blend of North African folk music. It has a rousing climax, with a Tunisian folk tune.

Five years later, Saint-Saens was back on the African continent. This time, he had in mind an even bigger, more expansive work that really packed in a lot of the folk music and sounds of North Africa. The result was his grand and popular *Piano Concerto No. 5 in F Major* (1896). It quickly got the tag *"The Egyptian."* There is no mistaking why. The second movement begins loudly, with a big sound. This is quickly backed up by the piano, which taps out a theme based squarely on a <u>Nubian</u> love song. Saint-Saens heard the boatmen sing it during a cruise down the Nile. Near the end of the work, he pulls out all stops, with the piano and orchestra working overtime to create a colorful, free-flowing sound, complete with frogs and crickets, which serenaded him in a chorus of chirps on the banks of the Nile.

 **Recommended Listening**

Igor Stravinsky, *Ragtime for 11 Instruments*
Maurice Ravel, *Sonata No.2 for Violin and Piano*

I cite the examples of two better known black music notables of centuries past along with the willingness of Saint-
Saens to weave African themes into his piano concertos to
underscore a part that blacks played in the maturation and
development of pre-nineteenth century Western music,
solely as an opening tease. My aim in *It's Our Music Too The
Black Experience in Classical Music* is not to update a book
on blacks and classical music written four decades ago, or to
simply chronicle the names, dates, and performances of the
legions of blacks who have composed and performed classical music. There are many articles, anthologies, and even po-
etic novels such as poet Rita Dove's fictionalized account of
the Bridgetower and Beethoven saga, *Sonata Mulattica*, that
do that and provide excellent source material for identify-
ing those figures and lists of their works. There are blogs and
websites that list the names, works, and accomplishments of
African-American composers and performers as well as the
composers and performers of African ancestry, both past and
contemporary.

AfriClassical Blog, a companion to the website *AfriClas-
sical.com*, offers interesting biographical snapshots of many
black composers. A companion to this is *Black Opera and
Concert Singers: A Resource Book*, a rich compilation and history of more than 700 operas by black composers. The Center
for Black Music Research at Columbia College in Chicago has
a vast treasure trove of the scores, manuscripts, discography,
articles, books, and films on black classical composers, and
performers past and present.

The Center's index of categories gives an idea of just how vast their holdings are:

Orchestral and Instrumental Music: Collections

Orchestral and Instrumental Music:
 Individual Composers

Vocal and Choral Music, including Opera: Collections

Vocal and Choral Music, including Opera:
 Individual Composers

Piano Music: Collections

Piano Music: Individual Composers

Organ Music

## Recommended Listening

*The Black Composers Series.* 9-LP set. Works by 16 composers. The College Music Society CBS Special Products P19425-P19433 (1986). Originally issued in 1974.

This is not a book of black "firsts." Not that it couldn't be, since there are many of them in the history of the black experience in classical music. There are colorful, tragic, and triumphal stories behind each of them such as Justin Holland who wrote the first manuals for guitar techniques in the 1870s, *Holland's Comprehensive Method for Guitar*, and *Holland's Modern Method for Guitar*. Or, there's the first black opera company, the Colored American Opera Company formed in 1873 in Washington D.C. And there's the first black woman,

Camilla Williams, to be a cast member of an American Opera Company, the New York City Opera when she sang in Pucinini's *Madama Butterfly* in May, 1946. Simply listing the lengthy number of "firsts" by black classical composers and performers in getting their music played or performing with major symphonic orchestras and opera companies would in itself fill up a small book.

Neither is this meant to be a comprehensive, definitive or exhaustive study of the entire tapestry of the black experience in classical music; that's a massive project that awaits and requires the energy and efforts of many scholars and musicologists. The book is a fast paced, reader friendly, easy to understand look at just exactly what and how blacks have actually influenced the development, history, and structure of classical music in its major varied forms; opera, chamber pieces, symphonies, and concertos.

My intent is to tell how the greats from Beethoven and Mozart to the jazz influenced big name pieces by George Gershwin, Igor Stravinsky, Maurice Ravel, and Aaron Copland have borrowed from and paid homage to jazz, blues, ragtime, boogie woogie and Negro spirituals. Throughout, I recommend many pieces to listen to by the greats of classical music who were directly inspired by black musical forms, as well as the works of black composers who have written exceptional works that have influenced the works of other classical composers.

Finally, my aim in *It's Our Music Too: The Black Experience in Classical Music* is to tell how black performers such as

Roland Hayes brought his unique interpretations of German *leider.* How Marian Anderson and Jessye Norman brought their distinctive tones and vibrant, fresh renderings of, and subsequent path-breaking performances in, the major works of opera giants, Giuseppi Verdi and Richard Wagner. Their renderings greatly altered how these masters' works are heard today. Throughout, I will let the major critics, composers and performers tell in their words their appreciation of the major contribution blacks made to classical music.

It is no exaggeration to say that classical music does owe a debt to the black experience in classical music. Bridgetower, Blanke and Sancho are just some of the many countless examples of that. There are many others that you'll discover.

Joseph Bologne, Chevalier de Saint-Georges

CHAPTER 1

# More Than
# the Black Mozart

In 1778, the then twenty-two-year-old Wolfgang Amadeus Mozart was desperate to boost his career. He travelled to Paris, the place where musicians and performers went to get their name in lights, before the public, and most importantly, before those who counted most, the wealthy patrons of the arts. They were most notably, the royalty, and those attendant to them. Things didn't exactly work out for Mozart. He was mostly shunned. A peeved Mozart hit back and called the French "frightfully arrogant." He claimed that "they understand nothing about music." However, his stay there was not a total loss. During his six months in the city he made the acquaintance of the man who did have the ear and eye of the French royal court. This personage provided a lot of music for the entertainment and delight of the Queen, Marie Antoinette.

His stature as a top run classical composer and musician was well earned. He conducted one of the best orchestras in Europe—Le Concert des Amateurs. His storehouse of operas, symphonies, concertos, and ballets were popular and well received by both the royal court and the general public. In 1785, he was authorized by a French count to commission Franz Joseph Haydn (1732-1809) to compose the six new symphonies that history knows as Haydn's "Paris Symphonies." He would conduct the premiere of one of them, the *Symphony No. 82, "The Bear,"* in Paris in 1787.

The composer and performer in question, Joseph Bologne, Chevalier de Saint-Georges, was the son of a Guadeloupe plantation owner and an African slave girl. Because of his meeting with Mozart and the style of some of his works, he has sometimes been dubbed, "The Black Mozart," or *le Mozart Noir.* His father had brought him to Paris as a boy and made sure he got the best education possible. A good part of that included getting the best of the best in musical instruction and training. By the time he and Mozart met, a near broke and near homeless Mozart had eagerly accepted an invitation to stay at the palace of a wealthy musical patron. As it so happened, Saint-Georges also resided there.

Through the centuries, the speculation has been endless that Saint-Georges may have given Mozart at least a bit of the idea of making the infamous character named Monostatos, who is black in the opera many consider his best, and certainly his most popular, *Die Zauberflöte (The Magic Flute).* Monostatos, just so happens in the opera, is the rapacious buddy of the evil Queen, a queen that in the end mysteriously dies, just as the very real Queen, Marie Antoinette, meets her very un-mysterious fate on the guillotine during the French

Revolution. The violence and upheaval raged during that same period in the 1790s when the opera was premiered.

There is no speculation, however, on the short passage that Mozart quoted in the third movement of his *Sinfonia Concertante for Violin and Viola*. It came from Saint-Georges' *Concerto for Violin and Orchestra,* Op. 5, No. 2. The "quote" that Mozart lifted from Saint-Georges is significant not so much for its uniqueness but as a musical acknowledgement by Mozart of the impression the composer from which the passage was borrowed from had made on him. It was a common practice then for composers to "borrow" passages from the works of other composers of note.

This was simply Mozart's way of showing his appreciation of Saint-Georges. As a highly lauded composer and performer, Saint-Georges was no Mozart. Nor was he a Mozart imitator. However, he was a highly polished, skilled, creative and formidable composer with a prodigious output of concertos, symphonies and operas. As a concert virtuoso he showcased an original technique in performance playing that bridged the techniques of composers and violinists such as Vivaldi and Beethoven. This too marked him as a meaningful player in the continuing development of classical music.

It would take more than two centuries for Saint-Georges to get the recognition he deserved. It came in 2003 when Jeanne Lemond, founder and director of Tafelmusik Orchestra, recorded 17 cuts from his various symphonies, concertos, and excerpts from his ballets, in *Mozart Noir.* The same year a Canadian production company produced a made for TV film on Saint-George's life, *Le Mozart Noir*. It won a slew of awards. After that, Saint-Georges got a bit more airplay on classical music stations and turned up on a few concert bills.

## 🎧 Recommended Listening

Chevalier Saint-Georges, *Symphony No.1 in G Minor*
Mozart, *Monostatos, Aria, Act 11, The Magic Flute*

On May 18 1803, Beethoven wrote to a patron, "I do not hesitate to recommend to you the bearer, Herr Bridgetower, a very capable virtuoso who has a complete command of his instrument." A week later, Beethoven got his wish; namely to perform with George Bridgetower. Beethoven went much further than the spotty contact that Mozart had had with Saint-Georges. He collaborated with Bridgetower and publicly acknowledged his musical skill when he, at Bridgetower's urging, composed his *Violin Sonata No. 9 in A Major*. Beethoven fully intended to dedicate the work to him. If so, it would have carried the nomenclature of "the Bridgetower Sonata" for generations to come. Beethoven even plopped on the humorous title, *Sonata per un Mulattico Lunatico* on it. He meant no offense. It was merely another form of flattery.

It was at the Vienna performance of the sonata in 1803 that Beethoven leapt up and praised Bridgetower and then embraced him. The British ambassador, Archduke Rudolph, Prince Lichnowsky, Prince Lobkowitz, and other wealthy patrons of the arts were part of the stellar audience of luminaries and royalty that had assembled for the premiere of the new piece. Beethoven showed even more gratitude to Bridgetower for his performance when he handed him his tuning fork. It's an artifact that is on display today in the British Library.

Unfortunately, the story didn't have a happy ending. Both men were top-rate virtuoso performers, and both had strong temperaments and egos. Allegedly they parted ways over Bridgetower's purported insult of a female friend of Beethoven's. Bridgetower begged him not to withdraw his name from the dedication, to no avail. In a fit of pique, Beethoven renamed it the *Kreutzer Sonata,* after his other violin-playing pal, violin virtuoso Rudolphe Kreutzer. An unmoved Kreutzer later said the work was too difficult and never played it. Regardless, the sonata still bears his name today, instead of the man who inspired it and expertly performed it.

Even then, Bridgetower recognized his great personal loss as well as the loss to future listeners by not having his name on the piece. Shortly before his death he lamented to a researcher that it was his name that should be on the sonata, and it would be *his* name that would forever be known across Europe. It would be *his* name that would always be associated with it. Nonetheless, Bridgetower's name couldn't be totally erased from the work. Ironically, Beethoven saw to that.

The following text is from Beethoven's sketchbook in 1803: "Sonata per il Pianoforte ed uno violino obligato in uno stile molto concertante come d'un concerto." His affectionate dedication read: "Sonata mulattica composta per il mulatto Brischdauer (Bridgetower), gran pazzo e compositore mulattico" (Mulatto Sonata composed for the mulatto Bridgetower, great fool mulatto composer).

## INSIDE THE VIOLIN SONATA NO. 9 IN A MAJOR

The final movement of the work was originally written for another, earlier, sonata for violin and piano by Beethoven, the Op. 30, No. 1, in A major. Beethoven gave no key designation to the work. Although the work is usually titled as being in A major, the Austrian composer and music theoretician Gerhard Präsent has published articles indicating that the main key is in fact A minor. Präsent has revealed interesting connections to the 6th Violin Sonata, Op. 30/1, for which the third movement was originally composed, and he believes that the unusual opening bars for solo violin form a kind of transition from the earlier sonata (or from its structural material), supporting the belief that the acquisition of the finale of Op. 30/1 for the "Kreutzer" was a compositional intention—and not a result of lack of time, as long suspected. *From Wikipedia*

Bridgetower's sole claim to have a place as a prime influential figure in classical music's history hardly began or ended with Beethoven. In the years after his collaboration with Beethoven, he continued to pile on the accolades as one of Europe's premier concert violinists and as a teacher of piano and violin. Equally important, he added to the body of classical literature on the art and practice of the piano when he published a piano work entitled *Diatonica Armonica,* which was published in 1812 and dedicated to his pupils.

## Recommended Listening

George Bridgetower, *Henry: A ballad, for medium voice and piano*
Ludwig Beethoven, *Violin Sonata No. 9 in A Major*

"He still wants recognition & is far away the cleverest fellow going amongst the young men." These were indeed flattering words in September, 1898, coming from someone who was then Britain's most lionized composer. Sir Edward Elgar (1857-1934) felt the lofty compliment to the young and upcoming composer, Samuel Coleridge-Taylor (1875-1912) the son of an English woman and a father from Sierra Leone, was warranted. The top music critic of the day, August Jaeger, went even further and told Elgar that he thought Coleridge-Taylor was a "genius." Elgar didn't stop with platitudes. He eagerly recommended

Coleridge-Taylor to fill in for him with a work at the prestigious Three Choirs Festival, which dates from the eighteenth century. Still in existence, it brings together choirs from the English cities of Gloucester, Hereford and Worcester. The event, held in September, rotates between these cathedral cities.

Coleridge-Taylor premiered *Ballade in A Minor* (1898) at the festival. And with that Coleridge-Taylor now seemed poised to carry the mantle worn by Bridgetower as the other significant classical music performer and composer of color, who found prominence in Britain decades earlier.

The real breakthrough for Coleridge-Taylor came in 1898 with the premier of his seminal work *Hiawatha's Wedding Feast,* based on the poem by Henry Longfellow. His stock on the British music and international musical scene soared. The premier on November, 11 1898, at the Royal College of Music was considered an event of the day. Some of the top patrons of the arts in Britain attended. One of those in the audience was Sir Arthur Sullivan (of Gilbert and Sullivan fame) who was near death at the time. Like Elgar, he also raved about Coleridge-Taylor, "I'm always an ill man now, my boy, but I'm coming to hear your music to-night even if I have to be carried."

The appeal of the work was its intriguing and, at the time, fairly new wedding of folk themes in a light and tuneful choral setting with a straight line and continuous melody. It was a fun work, that was not frivolous, or slapdash, and had the grandiose orchestral sound that by then had become the staple of the great nineteenth century composers from Beethoven to Tchaikovsky. Another of Britain's top tier composers also joined in the praise after its premier. Sir Hubert Parry called the work and the event, "one of the most remarkable events in modern English musical history."

This was not hyperbole. For the next three decades the work was the staple piece in choral festivals and commemorative events for the royal family. Famed conductor and composer Sir Malcolm Sargent virtually made *Hiawatha's Wedding Feast* the stage work national anthem of British musical performances, even naming a chapter in one of his biographies, "The Wigwam Years." It was taken from one of the set pieces in the work. During those years, many of Britain's top leading classical and stage singers performed in the production. Coleridge-Taylor would write other works, travel widely and was feted at the White House by President Theodore Roosevelt in 1904. He later became a well-respected and sought after judge of musical works in Britain. However, *Hiawatha's Wedding Feast* would stand as a prime work that extended the bounds of folk, choral, and the stage in the classical repertoire.

## INSIDE HIAWATHA'S WEDDING FEAST

**The most celebrated setting of Longfellow's story was the cantata trilogy, The Song of Hiawatha (1898–1900), by the African-English composer Samuel Coleridge-Taylor. The first part, "Hiawatha's Wedding Feast" (Op. 30, No. 1), based on cantos 11–12 of the poem, was particu-**

larly famous for well over 50 years, receiving thousands of performances in the UK, the USA, Canada, New Zealand and South Africa. Though it slipped from popularity in recent years, revival performances continue. The initial work was followed by two additional oratorios which were equally popular: "The Death of Minnehaha" (Op. 30, No. 2), based on canto 20, and "Hiawatha's Departure" (Op. 30, No. 4), based on cantos 21–2. *From Wikipedia*

### Recommended Listening

Samuel Coleridge-Taylor, *Petite Suite de Concert*, Op. 77
Samuel Coleridge-Taylor, *Ballade for Orchestra*, Op. 33

"In the Negro melodies of America, I discover all that is needed for a great and noble school of music." Antonin Dvořák (1841-1904) later waffled and tried to say there was nothing of the Negro in his new symphony, *Symphony No. 9 in E Minor, "From the New World,"* (1893), but he knew better.

So did Henry "Harry" Thacker Burleigh (1866–1949). He did what few other blacks of the era could even hope to do when he accepted an offer at age twenty-six to enroll at one of America's most prestigious musical institutes, the National Conservatory of Music in New York then directed by Dvořák. He sang and played double-bass in the Conservatory orchestra. Burleigh struggled to make ends meet, so he worked for the school registrar as a handyman and janitor. Burleigh's labor as a cleaner and musician didn't go unnoticed. He soon caught the eye of Dvořák, who, in addition to directing the conservatory, was in the midst of an extended tour in the U.S. to compose and conduct and give instruction to America's crop of burgeoning young classical musicians. The relationship between the two soon developed into more than just the typical professor-student relationship. In his second year at the conservatory, Dvořák was writing to his family in Prague that his son, Otakar, "sat on Burleigh's lap during the orchestra's rehearsals and played the tympani."

Victor Herbert also took note of the strong tie between the two in his own letter in 1922 to Carl Engel, chief of the music division of the Library of Congress, "Dr. Dvořák was most kind and unaffected and took great interest in his pupils, one of which, Harry Burleigh, had the privilege of giving the Dr. some of the thematic material for his Symphony. ... I have seen this denied—but it is true."

Dvořák went further. He was so impressed with Burleigh that one day he asked him to sing for him after supper. Burleigh later noted, "I sang our Negro songs for him very often, and before he wrote his own themes, he filled himself with the spirit of the old spirituals." Through December, 1892, and in the coming months afterwards, Dvořák filled his sketchbook with eleven pages of American theme music. Burleigh later noted about those "themes," "I feel sure the composer caught this peculiarity of most of the slave songs from some that I sang to him; for he used to stop me and ask if that was the way the slaves sang." One of them was the ancient Negro Spiritual "Go Down Moses" that Burleigh said he sang for Dvořák and which he complimented him with the quip, "Burleigh, that is as great as a Beethoven theme."

In a candid moment, Dvořák acknowledged the spirit of the music and the musical sound that Burleigh sang to him. This unmistakably comes through at the beginning of each movement of his American String Quartet (1893). But to the world, it's the spirit and the music of Burleigh's days singing Negro spirituals to Dvořák that comes through clearly in the second movement of Dvořák's "From the New World" symphony. Its well-known Largo is in the melody of a Negro spiritual. It is often played as a stand-alone number. There's even much speculation that the flute theme that sounds a lot like the spiritual "Swing Low, Sweet Chariot" derived from one of the spirituals which Burleigh says that he sang to Dvořák.

It was only fitting that when the work was premiered at Carnegie Hall on December 16, 1893, many of Dvořák's students were there, including Burleigh. Dvořák sat beaming in a box of honor with one of his many African-American proteges at the school. The up and coming composer Maurice Arnold Strothotte. Dvořák repeatedly boasted that he had the greatest talent and potential as a classical composer. Another student whom Dvořák thought had a good feel for the classical sound was Will Marion Cook. He, in turn, would later serve as a mentor to Duke Ellington when Ellington blended classical music stylings in his famed orchestral suites in the 1930s and 1940s.

Later, one of Dvořák's pupils, William Arms Fisher, penned the words to the song "Goin' Home" to it. Fisher claimed, "...the lyric opening theme of the Largo (second movement) should spontaneously suggest the words 'Goin' home, goin' home' is natural enough, and that the lines that follow the melody should take the form of a Negro spiritual accords with the genesis of the symphony."

## 🎧 Recommended Listening

Maurice Arnold Strothotte, *Plantation Dances*, Op. 32
Antonin Dvořák, *Largo from Symphony No. 9 in E Minor*

## INSIDE THE NEW WORLD SYMPHONY

The New World Symphony's best-known melody surfaces in the "Largo" movement, with its aching English horn solo. It was later adapted into the song "Goin' Home" by Harry Burleigh, a black composer whom Dvořák befriended while in New York. But I'm always moved by the church-like chords that come before that now-famous tune. In a stroke of innovative genius, Dvořák brings these opening chords back at the climax of the finale, where all the melodies from the symphony, reappear, transformed by the journey. *From Marin Alsop's "Dvořák's Symphonic Journey to the 'New World' " NPR, April 18, 2008*

Dvořák was not the only European classical master to be intrigued by black music. "Personally I find jazz most interesting: the rhythms, the way the melodies are handled, the melodies themselves… and I urge you to take jazz seriously." French composer Maurice Ravel (1875-1937) was so captivated and intrigued by what he heard and saw of jazz and jazz musicians during his four month stay in the U.S. in 1928 that he proclaimed his school-boy enthusiasm for the jazz sound in the magazine, *Musical Digest*. Ravel, like so many in-crowd whites of that day wanted to watch the swaying, gyrating, hot bodies on the dance floor at Harlem's clubs and listen to the jazz and sounds of Harlem's big bands of the 1920s. He made the obligatory pilgrimage to the Savoy Ballroom in Harlem. There he caught some of the hottest jazz on the continent.

The thoroughly mesmerized Ravel made the rounds of other night spots, including Connie's Inn and the Cotton Club, to catch the young Duke Ellington and his orchestra. Ravel was so smitten with the jazz sounds that he traveled to New Orleans to hear more. By now he felt confident enough to even give a lecture in Houston, which turned out to be part homage to jazz and part admonition to Americans to embrace and appreciate a music widely considered an American original, "May this national American music of yours embody a great deal of the rich and diverting rhythm of your jazz, a great deal of the emotional expression in your blues, and a great deal of the sentiment and spirit characteristic of your popular melodies and songs, worthily deriving from, and in turn contributing to, a noble heritage in music."

Ravel was determined to do more than just exult in the music and talk about it. He wanted to incorporate it in a work. The idea soon took the form of a piano work, a concerto for piano and orchestra. It took two years because of interruptions to write another piano concerto. The *Piano Concerto for the Left Hand in D Major* which premiered in 1930 was a commissioned work. It contains some jazz markings. One critic, writing decades later, was more specific, "In this work, two themes are presented in the introduction, one of them "derived from jazz, with 'blue' notes and syncopation."

 **Recommended Listening**

Duke Ellington, *Take the "A" Train*
Maurice Ravel, *Piano Concerto for the Left Hand D Major*

However, the concerto that Ravel had in mind as his homage to jazz in a classical form took an additional year to finally complete after finishing the *Concerto for the Left Hand*. It premiered in January, 1932. It was a smash success and Ravel took his freshly-minted *Piano Concerto in G Major* on the road to 20 cities throughout Europe. Within weeks it made its way across the Atlantic and was immediately put on the concert bill by two of America's greatest conductors, Leopold Stokowski who premiered it with the Philadelphia Orchestra and Serge Koussevitzky with the Boston Symphony in April, 1932.

The jazz style, especially the improvisational quality that jazz musicians brought to their playing, was on full display in the work. The fire, the passion, and seeming spontaneity, interspersed with the gentle melodic, flowing rhythms, and in some spots even a waltz like passage, are very much in evidence. The concerto fulfilled Ravel's urge to express his enthusiasm for jazz in a classical form.

## Inside the Piano Concerto in G Major

The first movement opens with a single whip-crack, and what follows can be described as a blend of the Basque and Spanish sounds of Ravel's youth and the newer jazz styles he had become so fond of. Like many other concerti, the opening movement is written in the standard sonata-allegro form, but with considerably more emphasis placed on the exposition.

At 106 bars in length, the large exposition section contains most of the musical ideas presented in the first movement. After the opening whip-crack and snare drum roll, the piano is introduced, providing a methodical accompanying figure as the winds present the first subject. Soon, the piano stops and the orchestra roars to life with each section adding to the theme, eventually drifting into an eerie, dream-like statement from the piano. This soliloquy is short-lived as the orchestra reenters with a blues-influenced figure, shifting between major and minor modes. The second subject begins with an awkward dissonance (A♯ and B), but quickly establishes

**itself as a richly melodic section, reminiscent of Gershwin's Rhapsody in Blue.** *From Wikipedia*

Ravel was not the first, and certainly not the last of Europe's leading classical music composers of that era to be enraptured by the jazz sound and either write works that were strongly based on the jazz idiom or incorporate elements of jazz into their works. The 1920s and the 1930s would stand as the blossoming period when classical music discovered jazz and the blues, and jazz and the blues discovered classical music. They would have a sometimes happy, sometimes bumpy, but always intriguing relationship.

Samuel Coleridge-Taylor

CHAPTER 2

# Charlie Parker Meets Stravinsky

"I t is remote from me now, like the work of a sympathetic colleague I once knew well." Igor Stravinsky could be forgiven for his flippant, even dismissive, tone about a work that he had one time called one of his favorites from the 1940s. The work Stravinsky wrote off so casually as something that had scant meaning to his long and world renowned musical career was the *Ebony Concerto* (1945). This is the same Stravinsky who would later exclaim, "The jazz performers I most admired at that time were Art Tatum, Charlie Parker, and the guitarist Charles Christian. And blues meant African culture to me."

Stravinsky may have been disingenuous in his later view of his unabashed jazz piece for the classical concert hall, but by the time the work was performed, he was well-versed on the huge impact that jazz had by then on classical composers. A decade before Maurice Ravel made his American tour in the 1920s and became a passionate enthusiast for jazz, Stravinsky in 1918, and five years after the riotous premier of his transformative, *The Rite of Spring* (1913), had his first awakening about jazz and the possible ways it could be woven into a classical work.

That year, the famed Swiss conductor Ernest Ansermet gave Stravinsky some scattered parts and piano pieces based on jazz and ragtime that he had gotten during his tour of the U.S. conducting Sergei Diaghilev's *Ballets Russes*. He was obviously impressed enough with the sound that he thought that Stravinsky, considered then the supreme innovator in the classical world, would also see some potential in the music for a classical work. His instincts proved correct. Stravinsky went to work and within a year's time penned three works, the *Piano-rag, Ragtime for 11 Instruments*, and a jazz influenced movement in his ballet, *L'Histoire du Soldat*'s (1918).

During the decades of the 1920s and 1930s, Gershwin took the musical world by storm with his big, brash, jazz rhythmic *Piano Concerto in F major* (1925) and his orchestral work, *An American in Paris* (1928), described as a "jazz symphonic poem." At the same time, Stravinsky was content only on occasion to include bits of jazz, blues and boogie woogie in his works.

## Recommended Listening

Malcolm Arnold, *Concerto No. 2 for Clarinet and Orchestra*, Op. 115
Paul Hindemith, *Suite fur Klavier*

By the 1940s, things were different. Judging from his complimentary remarks about the jazz greats of that day, Charlie Parker and Art Tatum, Stravinsky had been listening to the jazz artists and the bands of that era. So it was no surprise when he was approached about a commission to write a piece for the Woody Herman jazz band and an orchestra. The concerto he had in mind would be jazz based, with a nod to the blues too. He made it clear that the title of the work, the *Ebony Concerto* referred to Africa because, as he insisted, this meant "blues and jazz culture."

The work premiered at Carnegie Hall in February, 1946. The reviews were hardly earth shaking, since some felt Stravinsky's notion of a jazz based work didn't have the fire of the jazzy works by Ravel or Gershwin.

This wasn't surprising since Stravinsky was first and foremost a classical composer, and as most classical musical players and composers, he had a sometimes tortuous time trying to weave authentic jazz inflections in his work. The *Ebony Concerto*, however, still took its place among the long list of works that would bring jazz, in whatever way the composer chose, to the classical world.

## INSIDE THE EBONY CONCERTO

On August 19, 1946, the day after performing the piece together on a "Columbia Workshop" national broadcast, Herman and Stravinsky recorded the concerto in Hollywood, California. In the late 1950s Herman made a second, stereo recording in the Belock Recording Studio at Bayside New York, calling it a "very delicate and a very sad piece". Stravinsky felt that the jazz musicians would have a hard time with the various time signatures. Saxophonist Flip Phillips said "during the rehearsal ... there was a passage I had to play there and I was playing it soft, and Stravinsky said 'Play it, here I am!' and I blew it louder and he threw me a kiss'!" *From Wikipedia*

Stravinsky, though, didn't just give Charlie Parker a perfunctory mention for effect. Five years later, in 1951, he and his entourage booked a front page table one night at New York's top jazz club, Birdland. Parker and his quintet were playing that night. Midway through his set, Parker, without breaking stride, interjected the opening of Stravinsky's *Firebird Suite* in one of his numbers and then smoothly eased back into the number. Stravinsky roared with laughter, pounded his glass on the table, splattered the liquor and ice cubs over those at the next table. An impervious Parker continued to play, his musical stride unbroken. There's even a story that Parker tried to actually visit Stravinsky at his Los Angeles home. However, Stravinsky was slow in coming to the door and Parker left. If there's truth to this story this is another of musical lore's tantalizing, "what ifs."

## Recommended Listening

Darius Milhaud, *Trois Rag Caprices, for Piano,* Op. *78*
Leonard Bernstein, *Symphony No. 2, The Age of Anxiety*

The path that jazz, blues, ragtime, boogie woogie took to the classical world from the turn of the twentieth century through the first decades of the century was a two-way street. It had as much to do with the great classical composers such as Ravel and Stravinsky coming to the U.S. and hearing and studying the music, as it did with black musicians studying and taking up residence in Europe. As early as the close of World War I, Louis Mitchell and his Jazz Kings, the Original Dixieland Jazz Band and Sidney Bechet had performed in Paris and London and other European cities.

By the 1930s, legions of black musicians had made the trek across the pond and performed at clubs and night spots from Paris to Moscow. Louis Armstrong, Duke Ellington, Benny Carter, and Coleman Hawkins appeared at various times at European clubs. Other aspiring black composers and performers were studying at some of Europe's most prestigious musical academies under the tutelage of some of Europe's greatest composers, conductors and concert musicians.

This had a huge effect. French composer Claude Debussy (1862-1918) was so smitten with the cakewalk and ragtime and jazz that he included their rhythms in the last of the six movements of his *Children's Corner Suite*, written between 1906 and 1908. It's known as *Golliwogg's Cake-walk*. Golliwogs were popular kid's dolls in that day. What made them unique was that they were black characters, with red pants, red bow ties and wild, frizzy hair. The dolls mimicked the look of black minstrels. And when minstrels clowned, shuffled, and strutted for white audiences, they almost always were accompanied by banjo music. Debussy did the same in his cakewalk. There are banjo imitations in it, and the sound is of a dance or strut. The cake in the "cakewalk" was the prize awarded to the dancer who performed the fanciest, showiest, and most elaborate steps won. He took the cake.

Four years later Darius Milhaud (1892-1974) and Paul Hindemith (1895-1963) incorporated jazz rhythms in their works. In Milhaud's case, he used the structure of jazz, swing and the New Orleans Dixieland sound, and instrumentation in his twenty-minute ballet which was based on African folk mythology, *La' creation du monde* (1923).

To ensure that he got it right, he made the obligatory trek to Harlem in 1923 in tow with Gershwin to hear what Gershwin described to him as "real jazz."

## INSIDE LA' CREATION DU MONDE

**When Milhaud first heard an American jazz band in London (1920), he was reportedly so captivated that he took off to New York City to spend time in clubs and bars, visit Harlem and mingle with jazz musicians. After returning to France, Milhaud began to write in what he called a jazz idiom. He chose to color his music with bluesy**

turns of harmony and melody, swinging climaxes, and stomping rhythms. **Jazz influences appear in many of his compositions, but this ballet was the first opportunity to express his new passion; even the instrumental grouping also draws on his memories of New York City: "In some of the shows," Milhaud noted, "the singers were accompanied by flute, clarinet, trumpets, trombone, a complicated percussion section played by just one man, piano and string quartet."** *From Wikipedia*

At first glance, one spot in Europe that seemed absolutely, and wholly out of character for jazz and classical music to have any chance at a musical synthesis during this period was the Soviet Union. This was the hard line, totalitarian era of Joseph Stalin. The Russian dictator's rule was despotic and iron-clad. That despotism was absolute in politics and culture. Russian composers literally took their lives in their hands if they did not toe the party line that dictated what kind of music could be written and played. The line was that music must project "socialist realism," defined as a happy image of the toiling workers and masses in a Soviet socialist paradise. Further, it must inspire workers in their supposed ongoing struggle against capitalism.

Russia's eminent composer Dmitri Shostakovich (1906-1972) was not exempt from this artistic straight-jacket. By the 1930s, even for a ruthless totalitarian regime, the appeal of jazz proved irresistible. For a moment anyway, Stalin approved of jazz. The rulers and the party functionaries listened avidly and even danced to jazz records at private and some official functions. The Soviet bosses for a time protected and were patrons of Soviet jazz musicians. At the height of the Stalin terror years from 1936 to 1941, when the lid tightened on what could be written and played, jazz and jazz artists remained relatively unscathed. Stalin and the party bureaucrats even established the State Jazz Orchestra of the USSR. Stalin purportedly made sure that the jazz musicians were paid and paid well. The idea was to create a kind of national Soviet jazz. This trend wouldn't last, and within a few years, jazz was under vicious attack as a decadent western art form. Many of the jazz artists disappeared into the Gulags or were killed off during Stalin's purges. However, during the brief thaw, Shostakovich took the cue and composed two Jazz suites.

The two works are not regarded as anywhere near the best of Shostakovich's work. They have been called sugary, and superficial, at worst, and at best, light, inoffensive musical ditties. They were so lightly regarded, in fact, that The *Suite for Jazz Orchestra No. 2* which was written in 1938 for the newly founded State Jazz Orchestra and premiered the same year on Moscow Radio by the orchestra was lost during World War II. It would take sixty-one years for a piano score of the work to be found. The bigger point of the story of this short lived episode of jazz and classical music's fusion in Russia is that even in one of history's brutal and murderous totalitarian states, the two musical forms found a place together.

**Recommended Listening**

Dimitri Shostakovich, *Jazz Suite, No. 1*
Dimitri Shostakovich, *Jazz Suite, No, 2*

"**N**o new themes came to me, but I worked on the thematic material already in my mind and tried to conceive the composition as a whole. I heard it as a sort of musical kaleidoscope of America, of our vast melting pot, of our unduplicated national pep, of our metropolitan madness." With those words, George Gershwin announced what came first to his mind, and then later to the world. This was the genesis of what would become the universally recognized near perfect synthesis of jazz and classical music. The composition that Gershwin spoke of was *Rhapsody in Blue*.

He left no doubt that jazz would be central to the work by placing in the title "for jazz band and piano." The work was commissioned by jazz band leader Paul Whiteman. With the commission in hand and the jazz concept firmly rooted in mind, it didn't take Gershwin long to finish the work, about four weeks. At the premier in February 1924, many of classical music's notables were present, including Russian composer Sergei Rachmaninoff, now transplanted to the U.S. *Rhapsody* has been analyzed and re-analyzed countless times since its world premier in 1924. The general critical consensus is that with its incorporation of the complex rhythm and dynamism, Gershwin not only formally cemented the marriage of jazz and classical music in the piece, but provided a template for other classical composers of the era to mix jazz and classical music in a work.

## INSIDE RHAPSODY IN BLUE

The Rhapsody was performed by Whiteman's band, with an added section of string players, and George Gershwin on piano. Gershwin decided to keep his options open as to when Whiteman would bring in the orchestra and he did not write down one of the pages for solo piano, with only the words "Wait for nod" scrawled by Ferdie Grofé on the band score. Gershwin improvised some of what he was playing, and he did not write out the piano part until after the performance, so it is unknown exactly how the original Rhapsody sounded.

The opening clarinet glissando came into being during rehearsal when; "... as a joke on Gershwin, [Ross] Gorman (Whiteman's virtuoso clarinetist) played the opening measure with a noticeable glissando, adding what he considered a humorous touch to the passage. Reacting favourably to Gorman's whimsy, Gershwin asked him to perform the opening measure that way at the concert and to add as much of a 'wail' as possible." *From Wikipedia*

Gershwin adhered to the notion that jazz was a valued part of American music, that more often than not had been trashed or marginalized by mainstream musicians, and that it was important to change that. Gershwin did not work in isolation. He was good friends with the African-American musician and composer James P. Johnson (1894-1955) who had studied the European piano tradition with Bruto Giannini, an Italian voice and music instructor. Johnson wrote musicals, orchestral works, and even an opera. Gershwin was so impressed with his work that he based rhythms of the first movement of his *Concerto in F* on Johnson's *Charleston*. Gershwin almost certainly had the opportunity and occasion to exchange musical ideas with Johnson.

In *An American in Paris* (1928), and in his best-known musical gem, the opera, *Porgy and Bess*, he wove into them the jazz rhythms and tonality along with the popular songs of that time. He made it clear that his mission was to bind jazz and popular American music, "true music must reflect the thought and aspirations of the people and time. My people are Americans. My time is today." More on *Porgy* later.

 **Recommended Listening**

Kurt Weill, *The Threepenny Opera*
Walter Piston, *Symphony No. 5*
James P. Johnson, *Keep Shufflin, Harlem Symphony*

It could hardly be called imitation when Duke Ellington penned his own much shortened musical evocation of how he saw black life during this period. Ellington was asked to provide the music for the all-black 1935 musical film, *Symphony in Black: A Rhapsody of Negro Life* starring Billie Holliday. It was a first for Holliday, Ellington, and Paramount Pictures, which distributed the film.

But it was the music that caught the eyes and ears of the public. Ellington divided the music into four parts to correspond to a standard four movement symphony. He titled it *A Rhapsody of Negro Life*. It had all the trappings of a major operatic work, exactly as *Porgy*, mixed blues, jazz, folk, with a classical flavor. Unlike *Porgy* and other Ellington works that are today considered Ellington classics, the Symphony quickly disappeared. Parts of it were cannibalized and later turned up in other Ellington works. However, the work had the lasting imprint of a classically formatted jazz work that if more fully developed could have easily been a companion counterpart to Gershwin's *Porgy and Rhapsody in Blue*. It was concert-style popular music that was part of the tradition of works that orchestras produced for the theater and stage and musicals in the 1930s and afterwards.

✶ ✶ ✶ ✶ ✶

Aaron Copland was no Gershwin, meaning that he had no special mission to move jazz to a central place in classical music. Unlike Gershwin, Copland came to jazz much later, two decades later to be exact, than Gershwin. Still, he came, and when he got the request in 1947 from America's best known band leader and clarinetist, Benny Goodman to write a work with an explicit jazz theme for the clarinet and or-chestra, Copland dived in. He took what amounted to a crash course in listening to Goodman and other jazz pieces to get the feel and sense of jazz music.

It took three years before his *Concerto for Clarinet and Orchestra* (1948), conducted by Fritz Reiner and the NBC Or-chestra, was finally unveiled at a premier in 1950. Copland's splice of jazz with the classical sound came through with force and vigor in the second movement of the work. Critics took special note of the offbeat patterns and "syncopations" that are the trademarks of jazz. Copland had done his home-work on Goodman's fiery jazz improvisational style and em-bedded that in the piece. Copland punctuated all of that with some of the sounds of the Charleston and the boogie woogie.

Copland's later insight into the structure of the work and the instrumentation it uses tells much about how he saw jazz and how jazz had come fully of age in the works of America's classical music composers, "I did not have a large battery of percussion to achieve jazzy effects, so I used slap-ping basses and whacking harp sounds to simulate them. The Clarinet Concerto ends with a fairly elaborate coda in C ma-jor that finishes off with a clarinet glissando—or "smear" in jazz lingo."

Copland's *Concerto for Clarinet and Orchestra*, Ravel's *Piano Concerto for the Left Hand* and *Piano Concerto in G*, and Gershwin's *Rhapsody in Blue*, and in the later years New York Philharmonic conductor and composer, Leonard Bern-stein (1918-1990) are still the best known of the classical composers who blended jazz with the classics. In the late 1940s, Bernstein captured some of the feel and sound of jazz in his *Symphony No. 2, The Age of Anxiety* (1949), and his most popular musical *West Side Story* (1961). He also lectured on and conducted a series that included recordings of *St. Louis Blues* and *Dialogues for Jazz.*

By 1956, Bernstein had become thoroughly intrigued with the form and structure of jazz and the possibilities it presented to further cross-pollinate classical music. In his missionary like zeal for jazz, Bernstein was determined to spread the gospel on jazz far and wide. He had a ready-made platform on CBS's Omnibus TV program. Bernstein's popular series of lectures on the inner structure of the major symphonies had already drawn a big viewing audience.

At the time, he was working on *West Side Story,* so he was poised to take on jazz. "I love it because it's an original kind of emotional expression," he noted, "in that it is never wholly sad or wholly happy." He then set out to dissect the music of some of the top jazz and blues performers of the era, such as Louis Armstrong, Miles Davis, Buck Clayton and Bessie Smith. In a near hour long lecture, he ranged over dissonance, rhythm, and the African origins of the music. In that relatively short period, Bernstein succeeded in moving jazz, as much of the general public saw it, from the narrow confines of the nightclub set to the hallowed halls of the classical music concert hall.

Gershwin, Ravel, Copland, and Bernstein were, by far, the best known proponents to varying degrees of mixing jazz into classical music but they were hardly alone. *Wikipedia* lists twenty-eight well-known classical composers who have explicitly used jazz themes, rhythms, tempos, and even complete jazz forms in their compositions.

 **Recommended Listening**

Arthur Honegger, *Concerto for Cello and Orchestra*
Martin Gould, *Chorale and Fugue in Jazz*

Classical music composers embraced jazz with varying degrees of skill and enthusiasm. They used both the styling and the instruments unique to jazz such as the saxophone and clarinet in their works. However, the instrument that is the oldest and most widely used of all in music, and that certainly includes classical music, is the voice. A foundation of Western classical music is the use of the voice in its oldest form, the opera. This is the area of classical music where the black experience has also had a profound impact. The impact has extended even into how the great masters of opera have dug deep and based operas on non-European themes and story lines and cast black figures as major characters in their operas. The man who is universally synonymous with opera, Giuseppi Verdi, had his own term for this phenomena. He called one of his master works, *Otello*, his "chocolate scheme."

William Grant Still

CHAPTER 3

# The Chocolate Scheme

In August, 1879, Giuseppe Verdi wrote to his publisher Giulio Ricordi that he considered his stage rendition of Shakesperare's *Otello* a "chocolate scheme." It was intended as a complaint. Since a very reluctant Verdi, only after the relentless prodding of Ricordi, had agreed to compose the opera. Verdi may have found the task not to his taste, but the mere fact that he did it, moved one of the most famed black characters in Western literature, Shakespeare's blackamoor, Othello, literally to the center stage in classical music. It was not the first time that Verdi had anchored an opera on a non-white character. That distinction went to Verdi's signature work, *Aida*. She is the Ethiopian lover of an Egyptian warrior whose quest was to rescue her and fend off and save the country from the invading armies from Ethiopia.

Verdi's *Aida* provides a glimpse of Egypt, an African country, through the eyes of a European. It was this allure and fascination with non-European culture and societies that awed and fascinated Verdi as it did Mozart and Rossini, who also filled their operas with black characters, slaves, concubines, and dancers. Verdi did his homework and had his publisher scrape together as much scholarly material as he could get on Egyptian society and religious practices.

*Aida* was premiered in Cairo in 1871. In the century and a half since, it has become a world renowned crowd pleaser and ranks as one of the professional and dramatic standards by which opera productions are judged.

Now that Verdi based his great opera on the plight and travails of a black character, the question was just when a major opera company would cast a black diva in the role of *Aida* in a major stage production? The answer to that would have to wait for more than a half century after the production's Cairo premier. The breakthrough finally came in 1933 when Caterina Jarboro got the coveted part in a production staged by the Chicago Opera Company. Critics heaped praise on her performance in New York. More importantly, her singing style was amply noted and this would be a constant theme when black divas and black operatic performers were cast in the roles of principal opera characters. That theme was the unique quality of their singing style that elevated the operatic voice to another level. In short, their singing style was almost always touted as rich, full, expansive, and bursting with dramatic effect.

This is how critics repeatedly described the quality of the voice and presentation of the performer who has virtually become the definitive *Aida* of any generation, Leontyne Price. RCA records made the distinction official in an ad for its recording of Price's rendition of *Aida* when it quoted a Milan newspaper review of her performance that noted, "Our Verdi would have found her the ideal *Aida*."

## Recommended Listening

Giuseppi Verdi, *Aida*, Sir George Solti, Conductor, Opera del Teatgro dell'Opera di Roma, Leontyne Price as Aida
Giuseppi Verdi, *Otello*, James Levine, Conductor, National Philharmonic Orchestra

## INSIDE AIDA

**Antecedent: The Egyptians have captured and enslaved Aida, a Nubian princess.** An Egyptian military commander, Radamès, struggles to choose between his love for her and his loyalty to the Pharaoh. To complicate the story further, the Pharaoh's daughter Amneris is in love with Radamès, although he does not return her feelings.

**Scene 2: The lower portion of the stage shows the vault in the Temple of Vulcan; the upper portion represents the temple itself**

Radamès has been taken into the lower floor of the temple and sealed up in a dark vault, where he thinks that he is alone. As he hopes that Aida is in a safer place, he hears a sigh and then sees Aida. She has hidden herself in the vault in order to die with Radamès (Radamès and Aida: La fatal pietra sovra me si chiuse. / "The fatal stone now closes over me"). They accept their terrible fate (Radamès: Morir! Si pura e bella / "To die! So pure and lovely!") and bid farewell to Earth and its sorrows.[31] Above the vault in the temple of Vulcan, Amneris weeps and prays to the goddess Isis. In the vault below, Aida dies in Rad-

amès' arms. (Chorus, Aida, Radamès, Amneris: Immenso
Ftha / "Almighty Ptah.") *From Wikipedia*

"Because *Porgy and Bess* deals with Negro Life in America it brings to the operatic form elements that have never before appeared in the opera and I have adapted my method to
utilize the drama, the humor, the superstition, the religious
fervor, the dancing and the irrepressible high spirits of the
race. If doing this, I have created a new form, which combines
opera with theater, this new form has come quite naturally
out of the material."

This is how George Gershwin summed up for a *New York
Times* interviewer how and where he saw the place of *Porgy* in
American culture and how he was able to encapsulate it for
a general audience. Gershwin understood that black music
and life was vibrant, compelling, and multi-faceted. It had
the potential to be a huge attention getter in the arts world as
a stage production if packaged right. The story behind *Porgy*
is well known. It is based on the novel by playwright DuBose
Heyward.

Set in Charleston, South Carolina, at the turn of the
twentieth century in a small black enclave called Catfish Row,
it tells about Porgy, a crippled beggar who travels about in a
goat-drawn cart, and who falls in love with Bess, a woman of
uncertain reputation who is under the domination of a steve-
dore named Crown. Crown kills a Catfish Row inhabitant in
a craps game and flees. When he returns for Bess, he is killed
in a fight with Porgy. Porgy goes to jail, and Bess is enticed

to New York by a flashy gambler, Sportin' Life. At the opera's end, Porgy is heading to New York to search for her.

Porgy was more than a labor of love for Gershwin. It was hard work that stretched out over more than a year in 1934. It took that long for him to get the right words, nuances, and feeling in the songs that conveyed in an operatic work the pain and pathos of black life. Gershwin made it clear that he wanted American authenticity in the musical voice of Porgy. He combined folk (blues, spirituals, gospel), popular (blues, jazz, Tin Pan Alley), with the classical—the recitatives, the use of the academic fugue and canonic techniques, the aria, the leitmotif.

Unfortunately, Porgy had a generous sprinkle of the vicious and demeaning racial stereotypes that came with the racial turf in the 1930s. None was more offensive than the continued use of the word "nigger" throughout the opera. This sparked yet another profound shift in how black performers in an operatic performance would take the reins and reshape the texture and rendering of opera. The push back came in June, 1942, when Etta Moten in the role of Bess refused to use the "N word." Eva Jessye recalls:

"The word "nigger" occurred many times in the first scripts. Members did not like this but were afraid to object, that being the tenor of the times. But they could not bring themselves to speak it right out, so agreed to drown it out where ever and whenever it occurred in performance, thenceforth, disregarding all score markings or conductor's directions. The total ensemble would bombard the word with an avalanche of sounds, groans, screams . . . fit to raise the dead, to the puzzlement of the helpless conductor. Eventually the parts of the libretto where the word occurred was rewritten.

## INSIDE PORGY

From the outset, the opera's depiction of African-Americans attracted controversy. Problems with the racial aspects of the opera continue to this day. Virgil Thomson, a white American composer, stated that "Folklore subjects recounted by an outsider are only valid as long as the folk in question is unable to speak for itself, which is certainly not true of the American Negro in 1935." Duke Ellington stated "the times are here to debunk Gershwin's lampblack Negroisms." (Ellington's response to the 1952 Breen revival was, however, almost completely the opposite. His telegram to the producer read: "Your Porgy and Bess the super best, singing the gonest, acting the craziest, Gershwin the greatest.") Several of the members of the original cast later stated that they, too, had concerns that their characters might play into a stereotype that African-Americans lived in poverty, took drugs and solved their problems with their fists.

Over time, however, the opera gained acceptance from the opera community and some (though not all) in the African-American community. Maurice Peress stated in 2004 that "Porgy and Bess belongs as much to the black singer-actors who bring it to life as it does to the Heywards and the Gershwins." Indeed, Ira Gershwin stipulated that only blacks be allowed to play the lead roles when the opera was performed in the United States, launching the careers of several prominent opera singers.

That Gershwin sought to write a true jazz opera, and that he believed that Metropolitan Opera staff singers could never master the jazz idiom, but could instead only be sung by a black cast, seems to indicate he did not intend the work to belittle African-Americans. Some black singers were overjoyed at Gershwin's work going so far as to describe him as the "Abraham Lincoln of Negro music." The source of much of the racial controversy seems to arise from the miscegenation of Gershwin's jazz experience. Gershwin wrote Porgy through an idiom of jazz that was influenced by Western European opera traditions, African-American music, and Russian-Jewish music. *From Wikipedia*

*Porgy* quickly became an international cultural phenomenon. It gave European theater audiences its first real look at black life, and black music, filtered through the lens of a white American classical composer. Gershwin had succeeded with *Porgy* in exporting black music and culture to a global audience in a way black performers could not do during that era. It played to sold out audiences at Vienna's Volksopera and Milan's La Scala to adoring crowds. In World War II, the Danish Royal Opera premiered it in Copenhagen on March 23, 1943, with an all-white cast.

The opera was a great success, so much so that the Nazi occupiers warned the opera managers that an American work of any kind was not to their liking and that this one must be immediately withdrawn. Nevertheless, the opera was performed twenty-one more times to sold-out houses and with the theater surrounded by a cordon of Danish police. Finally, the Gestapo lost patience and said that if *Porgy and Bess* were shown one more time, the opera house would be blown up. The opera's managers ended the run. When the war was over, *Porgy and Bess* was quickly returned to the company's repertory.

*Porgy* was also the first American theatrical operatic venture to play in the Soviet Union. At one time or another, nearly every black performer has sang and/or danced in one of the varied productions of *Porgy and Bess*.

In the 1950s, *Porgy* had successful runs in Latin American, the Middle East, and Europe. But it was in Milan, Italy, at Milan's La Scala, the mecca of opera, that would prove to be the test. It passed with flying colors in February 1955 when it played there for a full week. The young Maya Angelou played the part of Ruby. She later noted:

"This was something unique: famous white American performers had appeared at La Scala, but never blacks, especially not a huge cast of blacks such as *Porgy* provided. Both audience and company were tense. Every member of the cast was coiled tight like a spring, wound taut for a shattering release. The moment the curtain opened, the singers pulled the elegant first-night audience into the harshness of black

Southern life. The love story unfolded with such tenderness that the singers wept visible tears. Time and again, the audience came to their feet, yelling and applauding. We had performed *Porgy and Bess* as never before, and if the La Scala patrons loved us, it was only fitting because we certainly performed as if we were in love with one another."

 **Recommended Listening**

George Gershwin, *Porgy and Bess*, with Ella Fitzgerald and Louis Armstrong
William Grant Still, *Troubled Island*, Based on the life of Jean Dessalines and the Haitian Revolution

No matter how many time *Porgy* has been staged, there would always be the two problems with the production. The language was one. It was still seen as racially demeaning by many. The other was whether the work is truly a classic opera. The much talked about and lauded 1976 unabridged revival of *Porgy* by the Houston Grand Opera provided an answer to both issues. The production was wildly popular, and appeared to truly reflect what Gershwin had in mind; namely the binding of two cultures and art forms, the black experience and classical opera. The opera company's artistic director Jack O'Brien noted, "The truth of the matter is, the music of 'Porgy and Bess' is as popular to the American ear as the music of Puccini is to Italian ears. But for some reason we've had a very difficult time seeing ourselves in this vast mirror of culture. America has a great deal of difficulty looking at its own culture with any confidence,"

The language issue was troubling. But in the end that was resolved as well, when research discovered that some of the slurred words that the black performers were required to speak and sang actually corresponded to the actual speech patterns of the Gullah dialect in the Carolinas. That took that issue off the table.

"You do us an honor to sing for us today and you do the human race an honor to exist." These were heady words coming from the composer and critic, Virgil Thomson. The occasion was the seventy-fifth birthday tribute to Roland Hayes (1887-1977) who virtually turned the German *lieder* into a state of the art experience for listeners. For decades, his name was synonymous with the *lieder*.

The German *lieder* is an emotive art song, a poem set to music, that expresses deep feeling, passions, and romantic love. The *lieder* is usually arranged for a single singer and piano. Two of the greatest composers, Beethoven, and especially Franz Schubert, wrote some of the most moving and expressive *lieder* in the song genre. Two of the best known examples are Schubert's "Der Tod und das Mädchen" *("Death and the Maiden")*, "Gretchen am Spinnrade" and *"Der Doppelgänger."*

The path that Hayes took to fame had was one all too familiar for black classical performers in the early decades of the twentieth century—one of denial, exclusion, doors closed, and opportunities lost. However, there were the triumphs too. Hayes scored many. His first major breakthrough came in December, 1923 when he sang at Town Hall in New York. This marked a turning point in the evolution of the German *lieder* through the vocal stylings and interpretation of an African-American singer. It was the force, intensity and passion that Hayes brought to the *lieder* that would soon become the recognized hallmark of African-American classical performers in opera, operettas, and other classical staged productions. After a Hayes recital of *lieder* songs one critic noted, "The fascinating thing in his art of singing is the intensity by which he lives through every song."

In the coming years, Hayes would sing before kings, queens, and the nobility of Europe. He would become the first black to sing with a major American orchestra, the Boston Symphony in 1923 under the direction of Pierre Monteux. Hayes brought two other transformative qualities to opera and classical music. The first was versatility. His repertoire in addition to his specialty, the *lieder,* included Old English folk songs, the songs of Dowland, Handel, Mozart, Schubert, Debussy, and Hugo Wolf were a major part of his repertoire along with Hayes' arrangements of "Aframerican" folk songs, Negro worksongs and spirituals.

The other quality was the strong sense that classical music was a big tent and that its flap must be fully opened to blacks. He shoved open the doors of the classical music concert hall to the other major black performers of that era, Marian Anderson (1897-1993) and Paul Robeson (1898-1976).

Each of them would, as with Hayes, be hailed for being the first black classical artists to make appearances with opera companies and stage companies that had previously barred black performers. In her celebrated appearance in the role of Ulrica in Verdi's opera *Un ballo en maschera* at the New York Metropolitan Opera in 1955, Anderson attained her "first" for black performers. This prompted the famed conductor Arturo Toscanini to quip that a voice like hers comes around only once in a century.

## INSIDE ROLAND HAYES

The Ellison-White Bureau Presents
Roland Hayes
Tenor
1936-37 Season Fourth Attraction
Portland Public Auditorium
Monday, December 7, 1936 8:30 PM
Program
I.
Pastorale "Alma del Core"........Antonio Caldara (1670-1736)
Adelaide................Beethoven
Sehnsucht................Beethoven
For Music................Franz
Walther's Prize Song, from Die Meistersinger............Wagner

Paul Robeson extended the bounds of classical music in another direction by blending black American folk music and opera into a unique blend of speech and song together. He scored his "first" with a recital at the Greenwich Village theater in April, 1925. Robeson also extended the bounds of folk, spiritual and classical music in yet another way by taking the music from the stage and the concert hall to mass outdoor arenas so "the people," as he loved to say, could hear it. In his view, this was music that could be both entertainment and a weapon to rally the poor, workers, and especially, blacks, to fight Jim Crow segregation, racial injustice and economic inequity in the 1930s and 1940s.

The feeling and intensity that Hayes, Anderson and Robeson and others that sing the great works of opera brought to the music and the public stage would be the hallmark of many black classical singers. "I believed there was a place in this world for a Negro concert artist," Hayes proudly said, "and I proved it." That he did.

 **Recommended Listening**

Roland Hayes, *The Art of Roland Hayes*, Six Centuries of Song, Reginald Boardman, Piano
Paul Robeson, "Ol' Man River," from *Showboat*

The *lieder* is one staple of German music. However, it is dwarfed in scale by the sheer immensity of German big scale opera. Richard Wagner (1813-83) made sure of that with his grand, gaudy, behemoth size operas that were stuffed with a fantasy land of Gods, knights, warriors, and maidens and based on epic, mythical stories and themes from German folklore. His *The Flying Dutchman, Parsifal, Tannhauser, Lo-*

*hengrin,* and his towering work, *Ring Cycle,* have been among the most frequently staged operas of all time for decades. Their performances wherever staged are almost always an event.

Wagner's works have so dominated operatic stages everywhere that an entire body of music literature and analysis exists on each one of them. His colorful life reads like an adventure novel; he was a scoundrel, philanderer, political rebel, fugitive, and notorious anti-Semite. Hitler's deification of him and his music has been well documented. Wagner is a cultural icon who is at the center of German cultural history and identity.

So, quite naturally there was some surprise when, in July, 1961, Wagner's grandson, Wieland Wagner, had a brainstorm. He decided to produce yet another production of Wagner's *Tannhauser* at Bayreuth. One of the divas that he invited to audition was the then twenty-four year-old Grace Bumbry, an African-American. When some in the German press got wind of this, they were apoplectic. They screamed that it was absolutely sacrilegious to even entertain the idea of a black singer, or as they put it, an *eine Schwarze,* in a Wagner opera.

Fortunately, the only voice that counted in the matter was Wieland's. He immediately cast her in the role of Venus in the production. Bumbry made history by becoming the first person of color ever to be cast in a major role at the prestigious Bayreuth Festspielhaus. The emphasis is on "major." Luranah Aldridge, the daughter of the great Shakesperian thespian, Ira Aldridge, was the first person of African descent to perform at Bayreuth as a Valkyrie in Wagner's *Ring Cycle* in 1896.

For her part, Bumbry gave a knockout performance in the role and received a wild thirty-minute standing ovation from the audience. After her performance, some in the hitherto hostile press went nuts reviling the *Die Schwarze* Venus." But even more interesting, Wieland shrugged it all off and said the old man would not have objected since he would want the best voice for the part, no matter her color. He would repeat that mantra, "I was looking for the best Venus in voice and appearance"—many times in interviews with the German press in the months afterwards.

Meanwhile two of the world's renowned African-American operatic divas, Leontyne Price and Jessye Norman, have made huge marks in the opera world by singing Wagner. Price's rendition of the *"Liebestod"* from *Tristan und Isolde*, which she sang at the Ravinia Festival in 1985, still draws countless raves today. It is hailed by many as one of the best versions of the song ever recorded. Meanwhile, Norman has feasted on Wagner, singing and recording many of the favorites from Wagner's major operas. Twenty-two of them are on the *The Jessye Norman Collection*.

### Recommended Listening

Richard Wagner, *Tannhäuser*, Bayreuth Festival Chorus and Orchestra, conductor Wolfgang Sawallisch with Grace Bumbry
Richard Wagner, *Jessye Norman Sings Wagner* (Decca Records)

## INSIDE TANNHAUSER

Venusberg (German: "Venus mountain") or Hörsel-
berg is the name of a mythical mountain in Germany sit-
uated between Gotha and Eisenach and celebrated
in German poetry. Caverns in the mountain housed the
court of Venus, goddess of love which was supposed to
be perfectly hidden from mortal men: to enter the Venusberg was to court eternal perdition. However, the legend-
ary knight Tannhäuser spent a year there worshipping
Venus and returned there after believing that he had
been denied forgiveness for his sins by Pope Urban IV;
this is described in the sixteenth-century Lied von dem
Danheüser, the principal source for Richard Wagner's
large three-act opera Tannhäuser (1845), which changes
a few story elements and is known for including a scandalous depiction of the revels of Venus's court in its first
scene. *From Wikipedia*

The stunning impact and success that black divas and
male performers such as Bumbry, Price, Norman, Anderson,
Robeson and Hayes had within the world of opera and the *lieder* songs has served as spur to many African-Americans to
write modern day opera works based on modern day struggles against racial injustice. The titles of these works by black
composers such as Anthony Davis's *X. The Life and Times of
Malcolm X* (1986), Nkeiru Okoye's *Harriet Tubman: When
I Crossed that Line to Freedom* (2010) and Richard Dainel-

pour's *Margaret Garner* (2005) are prime examples of how composers have used a classical format to tell a story of struggle and change.

It has also inspired many aspiring young black singers to envision a future for themselves in classical music. One opera admirer and lover was Dr. Martin Luther King, Jr. He was an opera buff. That's not as surprising as it may seem. His wife, Coretta Scott King, was a trained classical music singer during her years of study at the New England Conservatory of Music in Boston. One of her teachers was the noted Swedish-American soprano, Marie Sundelius. Ms. Sundelius performed in various stage productions at New York's Metropolitan Opera in the 1920s. One of those productions was Verdi's *Aida,* in which she was the voice of a priestess.

Scott King at times waxed nostalgically about her love of classical music. As she revealed in one interview: "In high school, I had a teacher who influenced me greatly. She exposed me to the world of classical music. Before then I had never heard classical music. She exposed me to the great composers of the world." In recognition of their great love of classical music, the Atlanta Symphony often includes classical works in its various events that commemorate the life of Coretta and Martin. Who knows, even Verdi might well have nodded his approval at that.

The impactful presence of black performers in opera, coupled with the fascination that non-European culture and characters, real and imagined, have held in the imagination of the great composers of opera and classical music, has spurred generations of blacks to explore and expand the dimension of classical music into the twenty-first century. It hasn't been an easy road for many of them to carve out a niche in that world. Yet, as with the black classical pioneers of the past, aspiring and polished classical music composers and performers of today have forged new trails in that world.

CHAPTER 4

# *From Bach to the Blues*

"The group performs five original themes based on classical music, along with four blues-oriented tunes. Although a touch lightweight, the music is enjoyable enough and certainly superior to most of Lewis' output in the 1970s and '80s." Although *Allmusic* reviewer Scott Yanow took a mild dig at the Ramsey Lewis trio for it being a "touch lightweight," the very fact that jazz keyboard virtuoso Lewis even dared to tackle Bach and Baroque classical in his 1964 recording of *From Bach to the Blues* itself was a near landmark moment in the history of jazz and classical music.

In tackling the music of the Baroque era, and naming it after the era's greatest composer, Johann Sebastian Bach (1685-1750), Lewis had also managed to prove the long held theory of some musicologists that indeed there was a closer connect between Baroque classical music and jazz than it seemed possible. A characteristic of Baroque music is the continuity of rhythm, melody and mood, and repetition; the same characteristics evident in much of jazz. There's also recurring passages for the orchestra and chorus in the Baroque form, and there are recurring passages in jazz as well.

Then there's the arrangement of instruments; with a Baroque piece there are two sections, the group of virtuoso soloists, and the orchestra section. In jazz, the section of solo instruments includes the clarinet, trumpet and trombone, comprising the front line section, and the rhythm section, including, the drums, bass, and piano. The other similarity is that a jazz number and a Baroque number have a strict, tight form in their composition.

Lewis, then, had flipped the musical coin with *From Bach to the Blues*. In the 1920s and 1930s, and at many points after, it was always the classical music greats, Gershwin, Ravel, Stravinsky, Copland, and others who raised musical eyebrows by their wholesale lift of jazz and blues themes for works that were hailed as a pioneering meld of the two musical forms. To many, they seemed to have as much to do with each other as the sun and the moon. However, when major conductors, production companies, and popular and respected white big band leaders, Paul Whiteman and Benny Goodman commissioned works from classical conductors for the concert stage or to showcase their musical dexterity, the snobs and the elitists grudgingly conceded that the two seemingly disparate musical forms could indeed reside comfortably in the same musical space.

It took more than forty years from Ravel and Gershwin's jazz-rooted piano concertos for Lewis to show that jazz and classical music was a two-way street. It wasn't accidental that

Lewis picked Bach to demonstrate that a jazz master could take the music of the grand master of the keyboard concerto and turn it into a sound that Bach might have recognized and approved. Bach displayed the full range of genres, styles, and forms of the day in his music. His music has always been considered by the experts as the closest thing to a complete package in encompassing harmony, counterpoint, melody, rhythm, and inventiveness. At the head of that list of those works is the *Goldberg Variations* (1741). The piano pieces have been the stuff of keyboard music that aspiring pianists have cut their teeth on almost from the time that Bach wrote and performed them.

Lewis's bold fusion of jazz and classical keyboard music was an important departure for jazz musicians in their continuing forays into classical music. But the counter trend of jazz musicians wanting to experiment with playing and recording classical music started before Lewis.

## Recommended Listening

Ramsey Lewis Trio, *From Bach to the Blues*, Argo Records
Modern Jazz Quartet, *Blues on Bach*, Atlantic Records

## INSIDE RAMSEY LEWIS'S "CLASSIC ENCOUNTER"

**No stranger to the world of the symphony—having studied classical music from a very early age—Lewis fus-**

es himself and his trio to the suave, plush forces of London's Philharmonia Orchestra, producing results that can be described as "to the manor born." Lewis' elegant soul stylings and classical arpeggios dovetail right into James Mack's full-scale symphonic arrangements, recorded at Abbey Road Studios in a lavish yet subtle way that transcends ordinary mood music. Yet mood music it is up to a point, for not much is allowed to disturb the warm Philharmonia blanket of sound, and though Lewis gets to display his fertile gospel chops on "Spiritual," he is a very polite American guest. One classical adaptation does find a place here; "The Earle of Salisbury Pavanne" by William Byrd (1543-1623) is turned into some kind of post-Fauré marmalade until a soft Latinish rhythmic underpinning arrives to save it. *From AllMusic Review of "Classic Encounter"*

Years before Lewis's classical foray, more than a few critics noted that several of Duke Ellington's most renowned works of the 1930s and 1940s, *Mood Indigo, Dusk, Reflections in D,* and *Creole Rhapsody,* blended distinctive elements of classical music characteristic of Debussy and Ravel. This was no surprise. Ellington was mentored by classical composer and acclaimed concert violinist Will Marion Cook who himself was one of Dvořák's students, Ellington spoke often of the influence of Cook and in telling of their association related, "Several times after I had played some tune I had written but not really completed, I would say, "Now dad (his fond name for him) what is the logical way to develop this theme? What direction should I take?" You know you should go to the conservatory," he would answer, "but since you won't, I'll tell you. First you find the logical way, and when you find it, avoid it, and let your inner self break through and guide you. Don't try to be anybody but yourself."

Ellington heeded Cook's advice.The distinctive tonal colors and imaginative instrumental combinations and variations that were the trademark characteristics of Stravinsky's *Petrushka* (1911) and the *Rite of Spring,* as well as his other works were exhibited in some of Ellington's works. Ellington's willingness to explore, improvise and mix jazz, blues, and swing and classical drew mixed, even hostile, reaction from some quarters. One of them was Ellington's record company, after the release of *Creole Rhapsody* (1931). Three decades later Ellington well remembered just how hostile the reaction was, "We just about got thrown off the label."

Thirty years later it was a different story. In October, 1962, Ellington was asked to compose a work for the opening of the Grace Cathedral in San Francisco in 1965. The church hierarchy wanted a special work to commemorate the occasion. This was a major test for him to bring the varied elements of the music spectrum together in a sacred setting and a sacred work. Ellington composed not one, but three sacred concerts, and the three contained a powerful mixture of jazz, blues, spiritual, in a classically formatted framework.

This was Ellington again at his best. He brought his acute sensibility and well-spring of knowledge about all musical forms to bear in a deeply moving, glowingly spiritual work. As one critic noted, "the concert taps into Ellington's roots in showbiz and African-American culture as well as his evidently deep religious faith, throwing it all together in the spirit of universality and sealing everything with the stamps of his musical signatures."

 **Recommended Listening**

Duke Ellington, *Concert of Sacred Music*
Will Marion Cook, *Overture to "In Dahomey"*

## INSIDE "IN DAHOMEY"

In Dahomey marked an important milestone in the evolution of the American musical comedy. Its composer Will Marion Cook combined the "high operetta style" he had studied with the relatively new form of ragtime in the finale "The Czar of Dixie." According to John Graziano, author of Black Theatre USA, it was "the first African-American show. The score made use of the "high operetta style" that synthesized successfully the various genres of American musical theatre popular at the beginning of the twentieth century—minstrelsy, vaudeville, comic opera, and musical comedy."

Significantly, the production of In Dahomey marked the first full-length African-American musical to be staged in an indoor venue (following the earlier success

**of Clorindy in a rooftop setting) on Broadway, premiering at the New York Theatre on February 18, 1903.** During its four-year tour, In Dahomey proved one of the most successful musical comedies of its era. The show helped make its composer, lyricist and leading performers household names. In Dahomey was the first black musical to have its score published (albeit in the UK, not the US).

**In Dahomey simultaneously builds on depictions of black characters, forging a significant shift in dominant representations of blacks in the theatre during its era and creating.**

**As the first show with an entirely African-American cast, In Dahomey is said to have been met with hostility. One New York Times report responded to the show by construing it as the initiation of a potential race war, signifying the level of anxiety possessed around the mobility of blacks during the era.** *From Wikipedia*

Ellington was the first in a line of jazz pianists who would write and play classical pieces. In 1953, Art Tatum did a solo rendition of Dvořák's *Humoresque* (1894) which was a short cycle of eight piano pieces. Tatum regarded as one of the most modern and unorthodox pianists of the time, put his novel, very impressionistic stamp on the playing of the work.

Tatum's playing also caught the ear of one of the twentieth century's greatest classical piano virtuosos, Vladimir Horowitz. The piano legend, as was true with the long line of classical composers such as Ravel and Gershwin, made frequent treks to New York jazz clubs to see and hear his jazz counterparts play. Horowitz was not just a listener out for a night out. He was intently studying and transcribing some of the music.     One of the numbers was Tatum's playing of the classic "Tea for Two." In a visit, Horowitz played it for Tatum. Tatum quickly returned the favor and played his version of it. An amazed Horowitz asked Tatum for the score he used. To Horowitz's shock, Tatum said there was no score. He had improvised it. Horowitz never forgot the session and what he heard. He later told an interviewer, "If Art Tatum took up classical music seriously, I'd quit my job the next day." Horowitz wasn't alone in gushing over the skill of Tatum's improvisation skills, the composers and pianists Sergei Rachmaninoff and Arthur Rubinstein were big Tatum fans. There's even a hint of Tatum's styling in Rachmaninoff's *Piano Concerto No 4 in G Minor* (1926).

The 1957 composition *Waltz for Debby* that was released as an album in 1962 by the classically trained pianist Bill Evans is described as an emotive interplay between the musicians in his trio and a model for piano play. There were marked elements of French composer Erik Satie (1866-1925), Ravel and Debussy in the work. The same year that Evans released his work, conductor and horn player, Gunther Schuller, who at one time was the principal hornist for the Cincinnati Symphony Orchestra and later the Metropolitan Opera Orchestra, thought that it was time to put a label on just exactly what jazz musicians were trying to accomplish with classical music. In other words, exactly what was this hybrid sound? It was neither purely classical, nor purely jazz. So since these were the principal forms of the music he was a practitioner of, it had to be a third form; a third stream. Thus he coined the name "Third Stream."

Schuller compiled a list of rules to explain mostly what the fusion of jazz and classical wasn't:

*It is not jazz with strings.*

*It is not jazz played on 'classical' instruments.*

*It is not classical music played by jazz players.*

*It is not inserting a bit of Ravel or Schoenberg between bebop changes, nor the reverse.*

*It is not jazz in fugal form.*

*It is not a fugue played by jazz players.*

*It is not designed to do away with jazz or classical music; it is just another option amongst many for today's creative musicians.*

With that, jazz musicians now had a term, a form, and a distinctive musical style that they didn't have to try and explain or justify to either the jazz or classical music purists who didn't see much merit in trying to muck up jazz and classical music by doing bad renditions of each.

However, this didn't totally satisfy some jazz musicians who still believed that jazz and classical music were not as far apart as the purists contended. The Stan Kenton Orchestra, for instance, in its *Malaga* (1972), borrowed heavily from the varied moods and textures employed by Stravinsky.

Jazz and classical music advocates were right, up to a point, in their assertion that jazz and classical music, apart from the Baroque, were seemingly incompatible. The two defining characteristics of jazz are its rhythm and improvisation. Yet jazz has no monopoly on improvisation. That's also a strong element in classical music. Bach, being a prime example, was one of the great improvisers with his keyboard music. Mozart and Beethoven also were masters of the improvisational art.

But what about rhythm? This is foundational to jazz, as Ellington famously said, "It don't mean a thing if it ain't got that swing." Few expect to hear the Ellington mantra about jazz in a Haydn or Mozart symphony. This is because there is no formula in classical composition for rhythm as heard in a jazz number. What rhythm there is in a symphony is short lived in a few bars. The exception to this such as Ravel's *Bolero* where there is a steady beat and rhythm is again the exception. One other example often cited is Beethoven's *Fifth Symphony*, where there is a dominant rhythm at points. But again this is the exception. The beat and rhythm in jazz is underscored by the drums which maintain a steady beat throughout a jazz piece. That's hardly the case in a symphony.

Also, while jazz has been annointed as the uniquely American musical form, it's also true that the melodies and harmonies of jazz are rooted squarely in European music. Jazz is certainly not, what one critic called, ad-libbed classical music with a swing beat. It is still at the core, free form, participatory and centered on the performer. Classical music is structured, autocratic, and centered on the composition. Yet, it shares enough with classical music in the improvisational aspect of it to have a strong appeal to jazz musicians, just as jazz had appeal to some classical music composers.

During this period, Charlie Mingus (1922-1979) also opted for a more formalistic style in his effort at a jazz and classical cross over. He went big with his *Epitaph* (1962). It is one the largest and longest works composed for a jazz orchestra with 30 musicians. It stretched out to over two hours. The enigmatic work confounded some who tried to position it somewhere between classical, jazz, and experimental. The classical connection, though, wasn't far from it. Schuller flatly said: "The only comparison I've ever been able to find is the great iconoclastic American composer Charles Ives."

## Recommended Listening

Phil Woods, *Sonata for Alto Saxophone and Piano*
Art Tatum, *Chopin's Valse in C Minor*

## INSIDE "EPITAPH"

After Mingus's death, the score to Epitaph was rediscovered by Andrew Homzy, director of the jazz program at Concordia University, Montreal. He had been invited by Sue Mingus to catalogue a trunkful of Mingus's handwritten charts and in the process had discovered a vast assortment of orchestral pages written by Mingus with measures numbered consecutively well into the thousands. After some investigation, Homzy realized what it was that he had found and eventually managed to reassemble the Epitaph score. At that point Homzy and Sue Mingus got in touch with Gunther Schuller, who put together an all-star orchestra to play this very demanding piece of music. However, despite the stellar cast that was assembled, problems were again encountered. Thirty years earlier, charts were being copied in the wings before the show. This time, the charts were all computerized, but the software was buggy and again charts were being sight-read at the last minute.

This was no mean feat. Epitaph resembles many other Mingus compositions in level of difficulty. Trumpeter Wynton Marsalis, pointing at a passage in the score said, "That looks like something you would find in anEtude Book... under 'Hard'." And conductor Gunther Schuller stated "The only comparison I've ever been able to find is the great iconoclastic American composer Charles Ives." Despite all these challenges, however, the concert, at Alice Tully Hall in New York's Lincoln Center in 1989, was a triumph, if ten years too late for Charles Mingus to enjoy it. *From Wikipedia*

The one constant in the cross over by jazz musicians to the classics is the influence that jazz greats such as Ellington, Evans, and Miles Davis had on them. They were not afraid to explore new bounds in their music and that inevitably led them to mix classical musical stylings at times in their works. For two of the leading jazz pianists, Chick Correa, and Keith Jarrett, Bach is the starting point. Both of them had played with Davis. Correa has done solo Bach on YouTube for pleasure and practice. It is a reflective, measured rendering with a strong element of improvisation. It is a textbook Bach keyboard variation piece. Correa has gone further and composed a piano concerto, an orchestral piece, and a string quartet. The pieces have been featured by the London Philharmonic orchestra and the Orion String Quartet.

Bach, however, is never far from their classical artistry. When asked whether his jazz playing influences his playing of Bach, Jarrett didn't hesitate,

"I don't know, but I do like what he said about playing beautifully, play the right note at the right time! In general, I like playing classical music in time. You can take liberties, of course, but still, the right note at the right time."

Jarrett too has gone far beyond Bach and has carved out a dual career as a classical pianist and composer, with a small but impressive series of classical works for both solo piano and orchestra.

 **Recommended Listening**

Keith Jarrett, *The Celestial Hawk,* ECM Records
Chick Correa, *Piano Concerto No. 1*

There was much more that Bach and other classical composers could take credit for in inspiring other top jazz musicians to play their works. In 2011, NPR listed five of the works of name classical composers that jazz groups played and recorded. Bach's *Fugue in A Minor* topped the list. The Modern Jazz Quartet, which through the 1960s had garnered accolades for its synthesis of classical and jazz music, recorded it in 1964. The famous Bach counterpoint is much in evidence in the recording. The following year saxophonist Wayne Shorter arranged Finnish composer Jean Sibelius's *Valse Triste*. Clarinetist Eddie Daniels followed this with a recording of French composer Erik Satie's *Gymnopedie No.1*

Satie was an interesting choice for another reason. He was about the most unorthodox, unconventional, anti-classical formalist composer of the late nineteenth and early twentieth century. He was the epitome of an *avant-garde* classical composer. And before Gershwin made his pilgrimage to Harlem and became enraptured with jazz, Satie had beat him to it and used elements of jazz and Ragtime in his works.

The modern day French jazz pianist Jacques Loussier also thought it fitting to record another work by a French composer. In this case, it is Debussy's best known and most recognizable work, *Clair de Lune* (1890).

The NPR list closes out of course with Bach. The recording this time shifted to south of the border with the Cuban group Tiempo Libre's album *Bach in Havana*, and featured Bach's *Gavotte* from his *French Suite No. 5 in G Major*. The group ramped up Bach with a danceable Latin beat.

"In 1958, during a segment of "The Subject of Jazz," says jazz pianist and educator Billy Taylor, "I was asked by composer Aaron Copland if jazz musicians ever improvised without previously deciding what melodies, harmonies, and rhythms they would use." Taylor has lectured and written voluminous pieces on the evolution, structure and impact of jazz globally and has flatly called it "America's classical music," But Taylor in this anecdote about his interaction with Copland, points to another interesting aspect of the musical meeting of jazz and classical music as seen from the jazz musician's view. That is the curiosity and even willingness to exchange ideas by jazz and classical composers with each other. Copland's curiosity was so stirred by Taylor's answer that he asked if he could hear an improvisation. Taylor obliged on the spot and improvised a piece which he liked so much he even gave it a title "Hurricane."

Copland was impressed. He said that it sounded exactly like a well-scored, modern abstract piece. The only difference was it had jazz rhythms. The impromptu session was even more instructive in that the musicians who played the improvised piece had not played together publicly, but were well-versed on the music played by the most original musicians of the day. Many of them had dabbled in the cross current of experimental and classical music forms.

Copland's inquiry about jazz's improvisations simply reiterated the importance of the characteristic element of improvisation that jazz has in common at least with Bach,

Beethoven, and Mozart who could, and often did, improvise in their works. This quality can be heard in the cross over playing of Bach and Mozart, et.al. by some of jazz's greatest virtuoso performers. Some of them saw enough in classical music to want to do more with the music, by adopting the formal, set piece structure of classical music in writing orchestral works, solo piano works, and quartets. The jazz artists have shown that just as some classical composers put jazz in their works, they could turn the table and put classical elements in their works. In doing this they have forged a common ground in two of the Western world's greatest and most divergent musical forms.

# CHAPTER 5

# The Invisible People?

"We are the invisible people in music," Kevin Scott, a thirty-seven-year old composer, paraphrased the title of Ralph Ellison's classic novel, the *Invisible Man*, to lament the near invisibility of black composers in the classical music concert halls. Scott was in Detroit in April, 1994, for a remarkable, even unprecedented, competition arranged under the auspices of the Detroit Symphony Orchestra. The three-day competition was to select and award a prize to a classical themed composition from the many compositions submitted by an array of black composers.

Scott's contention that African-Americans were the "invisible people" in classical music did not mean that blacks were not, and have not had, a significant part in influencing the works of some classical music composers through the years. He simply meant that in the modern era, there was a noticeable absence of blacks in classical music orchestras, and the works of black composers were equally absent from the concert bills of most major symphonies. The aim of the competition was in part to correct the situation by exploring the relation of race and music and, in part, to showcase and reward the works of the new breed black classical composers. The compositions that ultimately bagged the prizes typified the range of musical style, experience, focus, and experimentation within classical music. This was on full display in Donald E. Dillard's "Childhood Scenes," which won the competition. He painted an eclectic music picture that blended narration of the composer talking about his piano lessons, baseball games and church services. One composition recalled the 1893 Chicago World's Fair. Another was inspired by *Who's Afraid of Virginia Woolf.* And yet another was a politically inspired piece based on the upheavals in Haiti.

The pieces were edgy, moody, intensely personal, and even disjointed. They were bound together by their root in classical music forms. This was the same root that drove another black composer, who six decades before the Detroit competition smashed through one of classical music's hardest barriers. That is, to write a major symphonic work and get it performed by a major symphonic orchestra. This was not an easy task for William Grant Still (1895-1978).

## INSIDE THE DETROIT SYMPHONY ORCHESTRA

In 1978, Paul Freeman, along with local chorale director Brazeal Dennard, DSO board member, Dr. Arthur Johnson, and a group of community members and volunteers launched "Classical Roots," a program dedicated to showcasing the work of African-American composers, soloists, and conductors. Paul had long been a proponent of the work of African-American composers and recorded the definitive collection, The Black Composers Series, on CBS Records in the mid-1970s. The Classical Roots program, which continues to this day and was added to the orchestra's regular subscription schedule in 1989, touched people in a profound way. Dr. Johnson remembered one of the early performances: "The remarkable thing about the Classical Roots program is how deeply the music touches people. When I heard the orchestra play Adolphus Hailstork's Done Made My Vow at an early Classical Roots program, I turned to my wife and said, 'This is the first time that I felt a piece of music created from my own experience and it touched me as deeply as Beethoven's Ode to Joy.' It was exhilarating. *From Detroit Symphony Orchestra Case Study—The Color Barrier Is Broken*

The premier of William Grant Still's *Symphony No. 1 in A Flat*, the symphony the world knows as the *Afro-American Symphony* (1930) in 1931 by the Rochester Philharmonic Orchestra marked a true milestone in the evolution of classical music. The symphony meshes blues, jazz, and spirituals, punctuated by four dialect poems by the acclaimed black poet, Paul Laurence Dunbar as epigraphs in the symphony. Said Still, "I seek in the 'Afro-American Symphony' to portray not the higher type of colored American, but the sons of the soil, who still retain so many of the traits peculiar to their African forebears; who have not responded completely to the transforming effect of progress."

Since the debut of the symphony, Still has been the one, and sometimes the only, recognizable name among African-American classical music composers. His symphony gets most of the air and concert play for classical work by a black composer and is almost always played on classical music stations during Black History Month in February. That's another shame, as there is so much more available that William Grant Still produced that goes neglected and forgotten year after year. His work is still regarded as a solid addition to classical music. Among his works are: *Symphony in G minor* (1937); *Festive Overture* (1944); *Poem for Orchestra* (1944); and *Symphony No. 5, Western Hemisphere and A Southern Interlude,* opera (1942).

Still slightly pried open the concert hall door for a parade of other African-American classical composers whose work expanded the classical music genre and spanned all forms---symphonies, concertos, cantatas, operas, and chamber works. They are marked with rich harmonies, melodies, and stirring tempos such as: Ulysses Kay (1917-95), the operas *Jubilee* and *Frederick Douglass*; George Walker (1922), *String Quartet No. 1*; Florence Price (1887-1953), *Concerto in F*; Margaret Allison Bonds (1913-72), *The Negro Speaks of Rivers*, voice and piano (1942) and *The Ballad of the Brown King*, chorus, soloists, and orchestra (1954).

Ellington's *The Jazz Symphony* in the 1930s and the *Sa-*

*cred Concerts* thirty years later did raise eyebrows among classical music proponents. However, Duke had also brought his own unique and elegant blend of jazz, blues, and poetry to American classical music in the 1940s with his *Harlem: Suite from the River* and *Black, Brown, and Beige Suite* (1943); these are part of his *Four Symphonic Works* and our representative of Ellington's measured blend of jazz and the classics.

What is unique about the generation of black classical composers who have mixed jazz, blues, poetry, and story in their compositions is that they have also been willing to speak out, and speak out loudly, on the value of their works. And how those works are often on the cutting edge of classical sound and further widen the boundaries of classical music.

 **Recommended Listening**

Florence Price, *Symphony No. 1 in E Minor*
George Walker, *Concerto for Piano and Orchestra*

## INSIDE GEORGE WALKER'S ADDRESS FOR ORCHESTRA

The Address for Orchestra was Walker's first major orchestral work, dating from 1958–59, and was recorded by the Oakland Youth Orchestra for Desto Records. Changing meter defines the character of the first movement, which is dynamic and contrapuntal; the brief slow movement is, in contrast, static and monothematic. The finale starts

**with a hushed introduction before the passacaglia of the movement proper kicks in.** The curling, restless theme, over the course of 15 variations, gains in mettle and leads to a confident yet defiant climax. The Overture: In Praise of Folly, takes snippets from a variety of tunes ("America the Beautiful," "A Tisket, a Tasket," "Yankee Doodle," and several others) and manipulates them. Note, not "plays" with them, as this is rather a serious work, rather densely scored at times. *From ArkiviMusic The Source for Classical Music*

Some corners of the classical music world have recognized the importance of black musical forms and the cultural experience in the works of some noted composers. Yet, the eternal question still dangles: Is the classical music glass full or half empty for black composers? Just how much progress has been made in getting the attention they deserve measured by the frequency of the play of the works of black composers? That's the question that's been repeatedly asked in the eight plus decades since composer and pianist Florence Price had her "first" when she became the first black woman to have a work played by a major American orchestra when the Chicago Symphony premiered her *Symphony in E* a silky, placid work in June, 1933.

Even so, she still had to plead with Serge Koussevitzky, the conductor of the Boston Symphony Orchestra, to play any of her music. She knew why. "To begin with," she wrote in a 1943 letter, "I have two handicaps—those of sex and race.

I am a woman; and I have some Negro blood in my veins. I should like to be judged on merit alone." Eight decades later the Boston Symphony has not answered her plea and programmed any of her music.

Composer Thomas Jefferson (T.J.) Anderson undoubtedly knows well the agony and humiliation in the present period of having to plead for recognition. He told an interviewer that the one thing above all is that "we need exposure." He has been in the composing business dating back to Ellington's day. He's written over eighty works ranging from operas and symphonies to choral pieces, chamber music, and band music. One of his highly touted special commissioned works is *In Front of My Eyes: An Obama Celebration for Soprano, Flute (Piccolo and Alto Flute)* (2010). Anderson has been outspoken in challenging the classical world to lift the cloak of invisibility that shrouds African-American classical composers.

Anderson, though, also puts his finger on something else that makes and has made black musical forms and images at once both captivating to some of the biggest names in classical music and at the same time has provoked a distancing and its diminution. He notes that nearly all black composers have been avant-garde in how they have blended their music and attempted to integrate it into classical forms.

This ironically has led to a Catch-22. That is that a black composer and performer is ostracized and excluded from concert bills while at the same time composers hijack the varied black musical forms be it jazz (Gershwin and Ravel and

Dimitri Shostakovich, blues (Copland), ragtime (Stravinsky and Debussy) and spirituals (Dvořák) and infuse them in their works.

The younger black composers take a different approach to the struggle for recognition in the concert hall. They believe that their classical compositions can't and shouldn't be pigeonholed as "black music" that happens to appear here and there in a classical piece. "As an African-American composer," Jonathan Bailey Holland notes, "I have certain experiences that shaped who I am, and that I draw on as a composer,"

Holland with his mixed media, *avante garde* undulating tone poem *Shards of Serenity* (2013) has drawn raves the times it has been performed. Composer and musical scholar George Lewis has also raised more than a few eyebrows with his *"Memex" for Orchestra* (2014). This almost literally pummels the ear with sounds and instruments that blast notes from every conceivable direction. Lewis, though, has done more than stretch the outer limits of classical music with his trend setting work in electronics, he also has admonished the classical music world to recognize that this type of sound is yet another new addition to the music, and it must come without a color bar.

At a panel in London, he says, "They had these ready-made lineages all made up," he said with a laugh. "They had a black one for me, and they had a white one for the white guy on the panel. So it was like, 'Well, wait a minute.' They were very offended when I didn't put on the suit that didn't really fit." A white composer had spoken about the influence of R&B on his own music, Lewis said, and "it occurred to me that he knew a lot more about Bo Diddley than I did. Why couldn't that be a part of his lineage, and why couldn't Louis Andriessen be a part of mine?"

 **Recommended Listening**

George Lewis, *Anthem* for chamber ensemble with electronics
Jonathan Holland Bailey, *Equality*, Cincinnati Symphony Orchestra

## Inside George Lewis's Voyager

Voyager is a nonhierarchical, interactive musical environment that privileges improvisation. In Voyager, improvisors engage in dialogue with a computer-driven, interactive "virtual improvising orchestra." A computer program analyzes aspects of a human improvisor's performance in real time, using that analysis to guide an automatic composition (or, if you will, improvisation) program that generates both complex responses to the musicians playing and independent behavior that arises from its own internal processes.

This work, which is one of my most widely performed compositions, deals with the nature of music and, in particular, the processes by which improvising musicians produce it. These questions can encompass not only

**technological or music-theoretical interests but philosophical, political, cultural and social concerns as well. This is consistent with the instrumental dimension or tendency in African musical organization, or what Robert Farris Thomson identifies as "songs and dances of social allusion," one of several "ancient African organizing principles of song and dance that crossed the seas from the Old World to the New."** *From George Lewis, "Ways & Means: Too Many Notes: Computers, Complexity and Culture in Voyager," Leonardo Music Journal 10 (2000) 33-39*

There's also the frustrating cycle that has grown up within and without classical music regarding black composers. While black composers fight hard to get their compositions performed, they encounter resistance to get wider exposure of their works. Thus their selections from most concert bills insures that the almost lily-white concert halls that Bob Watt decried remain that way. This, in turn, feeds the perception that classical music is, and always has been, solely a music played and written by mostly European whites for whites.

Pianist Roy Eaton zeroed in on the damaging effect of the cycle: "Most African-American homes do not as a habit listen to classical music. They haven't been shown the possibility and also they don't see role models. That is something that has infuriated me—I was going to say 'irked,' but it's not 'irked'—it's infuriated me."

The key to breaking the cycle is to create and sustain institutions which provide resources to educate and train aspiring young black musicians in the classical music arts. The Detroit based Sphinx organization, founded in 1996, boldly states that its mission is to introduce, inspire and provide young musicians of color with professional training and performance opportunities in classical music. The issue, as always, is getting the classical music groups and artists interested enough to provide funding and support, and most importantly, access to the concert hall.

Acclaimed classical violinist and professor, Aaron Dworkin, the Sphinx founder, had no illusions about the immense challenge in attaining the goal of making diversity a reality in the classical music field. He knew that the first step was to dispel the great myth that blacks are not interested in or talented enough to have a successful career in the field. "At the beginning of this journey, some believed that the talent is not inherent in the communities of colour, relative to classical music. However, the myth is becoming successfully dispelled through the work of our amazing alumni." Thousands of young persons have gotten their first exposure to classical music through the organization. The next hurdle is to push, and prod symphony organizations to establish their own training and development programs and performance venues for these musicians.

His efforts, as well as those of other groups and individuals that are passionately devoted to promoting diversity in classical music, have paid dividends on many occasions. One especially memorable occasion was in June, 2015, when a group of third-graders at a Harlem public school, brought the house down when they sang the finale of Mozart's *Magic Flute.* The youngsters rehearsed with visiting artists from *Opera on Tap's* six week *Operaprogram.* After the performance, the students were asked how many loved opera. They all eagerly said, yes, and that the experience of singing and playing in the Mozart classic opened wide their discovery of the beauty and power of opera. It also gave them a sense of self-empowerment, in that they felt they were part of a professional company.

Black composers and performers, no matter what age, will slowly, but steadily continue to influence classical music in various ways with new imaginative forms such as storytelling, narration, and electronics woven into a classical musical score. This will help change the perception that classical music is the forbidden enclave that is the exclusive preserve of white males. This was the perception back in the time when talented blacks were rammed to the outer edges of the classical music world. Yet even then they were still there writing, performing, and stamping their special label on the music. The black classical composers of the twenty-first century will eventually burst out of that recess and become an integral part of the driving, inspiring, and creative force that has always been the trademark of classical music.

The Detroit Symphony sponsored competition in 1994, along with other similar competitions, and the work of organizations such as the Sphinx Organization has been essential. The willingness of some symphony groups to commission works by African-American composers too is a vital step toward providing an on-going platform on the big stage of classical music for up and coming composers. This is another exciting challenge for classical music in the twenty-first century.

Florence Price

# Conclusion

"I am convinced that the future music of this country must be founded on what are called Negro melodies. These can be the foundation of a serious and original school of composition, to be developed in the United States. These beautiful and varied themes are the product of the soil. They are the folk songs of America and your composers must turn to them." Antonin Dvořák made that pronouncement on the eve of the unveiling of his brand new symphony, "From the New World," in New York in 1893. He did exactly what he said in the symphony and directly incorporated the sound and rhythm of a black spiritual.

Four decades later, Alain Locke, in 1936 echoed Dvořák's sentiment when he wrote:

"The Negro has been the main source of America's popular music, and promises, as we shall see, to become one of the main sources of America's serious or classical music, at least that part which strives to be natively American and not derivative of European types of music."

Locke, a novelist, and widely recognized as one of the leading lights of the Harlem Renaissance of the 1930s, and Dvořák, recognized as one of the classical music world's greatest symphonic composers, came to the same conclusion. That is, that black music, whether it's jazz, blues, ragtime, boogie woogie, or the spirituals has provided source material and inspiration for the classical music world's great composers. Yet, this tells only part of the story of the influence black music and culture has had on classical music.

There's also the fascination by opera giants from Mozart to Verdi with black characters and themes they either put in their works or based their works on, as well as utilizing source material from Africa. There was the willingness of a classical composer of the Olympian stature of Beethoven to embrace literally and to recognize the musical virtuosity of George Bridgetower, and collaborate with him on an important work.

Then there's the repeated observation, recognition and praise by legions of music critics of the unique passion, intensity, and vibrancy that black opera and art song artists have brought to opera and the classical music stage. As composer and critic, Virgil Thomson once famously said, "Negro singers, as always, make opera credible, they never seem inappropriately cast for any musical style." This is exactly what spurred Wieland Wagner, the grandson of Richard Wagner, to break from the stodgy, staid, rigid, and bigoted ranks of Wagnerian opera, and cast the first black performer to play the leading role in Wagner's *Tannhauser* at one of the opera world's hallowed shrines, the Bayreuth festival.

## Inside Virgil Thomson's opera "Four Saints in Three Acts"

**It was at one of these performances that Thomson decided that his opera would feature an all-black cast of singers. "Four Saints in Three Acts" premiered in Hartford in early February1934, notably a year before George Gershwin's first, famous all-black production of Porgy and Bess. Even though Stein dissuaded Thomson from his initial ideas of putting the singers on stage in transparent costuming and white face-paint, the opera was nonetheless sufficiently scandalous enough with its black cast and unorthodox, non-narrative structure. However, news of its invitation-only premiere incited great anticipation among critics and the social elite. They were not disappointed, and the opera opened on Broadway later that month.** *From Wikipedia*

The real strength of classical music is that it has been able to continually expand, stretch, broaden, transform, bend, and even redefine itself through the centuries. In each of its phases of evolution, black performers and composers such as John Blanke and Ignatius Sancho in medieval and eighteenth century England added their music and compositions to the evolution. In the latter twentieth century and early twenty-first centuries, there are new trends that further broaden the traditional view of what's categorized as classical music. This now includes jazz, folk, and musicals, as well as music from other cultures, such as Asian, African, and Latin American. Despite these welcome changes, black composers and performers still fight a tough uphill battle to lift the shroud of invisibility that has enveloped them in the past and present. It's still a constant fight to get commissions for their works, training, and resources to cultivate young talent, and most importantly to gain access to perform in the major symphonies and opera productions. This is the key to insuring that the black experience still plays an integral part classical music.

## Recommended Listening

Ignatius Sancho, *Minuet No. 4 in F Major*

Dvořák recognized and acknowledged the artistic weight of black music, musicians and their culture before, during, and after he wrote the *New World Symphony*. Gershwin recognized and acknowledged its weight in his piano concertos and his stage musical, *Porgy*. The Detroit Symphony recognized the same weight and acknowledges it when it stages competitions to discover and encourage black classical composers.

The influence blacks have had on classical music is and has been both a reality and challenge. It's for precisely this reason that black classical composers and performers through the ages have said and proved in their works and performances that classical is our music, too. This is simply another way of saying that classical music is and always has been a big tent for all.

Grace Bumbry

# *Notes*

## Introduction

"John Blanke, "A Black Trumpeter In The Court of King Henry VIII," *The Black Presence in Britain, March 12, 2009,* www.blackpresence.co.uk/john-blanke/

Michael Ohajuru, "John Blanke, Henry VIII's Black Trumpeter, Petitions for a Back Dated Pay Increase," July 27, 2015, *Many Headed Monster. wordpress,* www.manyheaded-monster.wordpress.com/2015/07/27/john-blanke-henry-viiis-black-trumpeter-petitions-for-a-back-dated-pay-increase-2/

www.100greatblackbritons.com/bios/ignatious_sancho.html

## Chapter 1: More Than the Black Mozart

Jessica Duchen, "Chevalier de Saint-Georges: The man who got under Mozart's skin," *Independent,* February 7, 2016, www.independent.co.uk/arts-entertainment/classical/features/chevalier-de-saint-georges-the-man-who-got-under-mozarts-skin-a6859191.html

www.en.wikipedia.org/wiki/Chevalier_de_Saint-Georges

Roberta Hershenson, "A Swashbuckling Violinist, Fresh from the 1700s," *NY Times*, January 6, 2008, www.nytimes. com/2008/01/06/nyregion/nyregionspecial2/06bookwe. html?_r=0

Raoul Abdul, *Blacks in Classical Music*, (New York: Dodd, Mead, 1978) p.177

"George Bridgetower (1779-1860) and Beethoven: a troubled relationship," *Classic FM*, nd, www.classicfm.com/ composers/beethoven/guides/key-people-beethovens-music-and-life-george-bridge/

www.beethoven.ru/img/bridgetower.pdf

Ginny Burges, "Beethoven and Bridgetower: The Story Behind the Famous 'Kreutzer' Sonata," *Rhapsodyinwords*, February 8, 2016, www.rhapsodyinwords.com/2016/02/08/ beethoven-and-bridgetower-the-story-behind-the-famous-kreutzer-sonata/

www.bl.uk/onlinegallery/features/blackeuro/pdf/ coleridge.pdf

www.en.wikipedia.org/wiki/Samuel_Coleridge-Taylor

www.en.wikipedia.org/wiki/The_Song_of_Hiawatha_ (Coleridge-Taylor)

www.en.wikipedia.org/wiki/Harry_Burleigh#At_ the_National_Conservatory.2C_relation_with_Dvo.C5.99. C3.A1k

www.Dvořáknyc.org/african-american-influences

www.en.wikipedia.org/wiki/Maurice_Arnold_Stro-thotte

www.en.wikipedia.org/wiki/Lied

Raoul Abdul, *Blacks in Classical Music*, 74, 78

Kira Thurman, "Black Venus, White Bayreuth, Race and Sexuality and the Depoliticization of Wagner in Postwar West Germany," *German Studies*, 35.3, 2012, 607-626, www.academia.edu/2075599/Black_Venus_White_Bayreuth_Race_Sexuality_and_the_Depoliticization_of_Wagner_in_Postwar_West_Germany

Louise Burton, "Fascinatin' rhythm: When Ravel met Gershwin in Jazz Age New York," *CSO Sounds and Stories*, May 26, 2015, www.csosoundsandstories.org/fascinatin-rhythm-when-ravel-met-gershwin-in-jazz-age-new-york/

www.dsso.com/wp-content/uploads/2016/03/RAVEL-Piano-Concerto-in-G.pdf

Dave Baker, "The Influence of Jazz," NPR Online, nd, www.npr.org/programs/specials/milestones/990210.motm.jazz.html

Logan K. Young, "International Jazz Day: Igor Stravinsky—Jazz After Spring," *Classicalite*, April 30, 2013, www.classicalite.com/articles/1456/20130430/international-jazz-day-igor-stravinsky-spring.htm

www.en.wikipedia.org/wiki/Ebony_Concerto_(Stravinsky)

"Great Encounters #: When Charlie Parker played for Igor Stravinsky," *Jerry Jazz Musician*, April 29, 2004, www.jerryjazzmusician.com/2004/01/great-encounters-1-when-charlie-parker-played-for-igor-stravinsky/

"Jazz in The Soviet Union During The 1930s," *History Essay*, March 23, 2015, www.ukessays.com/essays/history/

jazz-in-the-soviet-union-during-the-1930s-history-essay.php

www.en.wikipedia.org/wiki/Symphony_in_Black

"Horowitz and Tatum—When Jazz and Classical Music Met," *Classical Music Blogspot*, July 25, 2012, www.classical-musicblogspot.com/horowitz-and-tatum-when-jazz-met-classical/

K. Stewart Meredith, "Jazz and Germany: The Exodus of Jazz and World War II," www.academia.edu/2402718/Jazz_and_Germany_The_Exodus_of_Jazz_and_World_War_II

www.en.wikipedia.org/wiki/Rhapsody_in_Blue

www.en.wikipedia.org/wiki/George_Gershwin

www.academia.edu/1601416/The_Nature_of_Aaron_Copland_s_Clarinet_Concerto

Abdul, *Blacks in Classical Music*, 128-130

"*What is Jazz?*: Leonard Bernstein's Introduction to the Great American Art Form (1956)," *Open Culture*, April 30, 2015, www.openculture.com/2015/04/leonard-bernsteins-introduction-to-jazz.html

## CHAPTER 3: THE CHOCOLATE SCHEME

www.en.wikipedia.org/wiki/Giuseppe_Verdi

Mena Mark Hanna, "Verdi's Egypt," *Huffington Post*, November 3, 2013, www.huffingtonpost.com/mena-mark-hanna-dphil/verdis-egypt_b_4196285.html

James Standifer, "The Tumultuous Life of Porgy and Bess," *Humanities*, Vol 18, No. 6, November-December, 1997, www.neh.gov/humanities/1997/novemberdecember/feature/the-tumultuous-life-porgy-and-bess

Kenneth Herman, 'Porgy And Bess' Production Story," *Los Angeles Times*, March 4, 1987, www.articles.latimes. com/1987-03-04/entertainment/ca-4562_1_san-diego-opera

Jason Victor Serinus, "The Artistry of Afraamerican Roland Hayes," *Classical Voice*, February 8, 2011, www.sfcv.org/ reviews/the-artistry-of-aframerican-roland-hayes

Alison Kinney, "As the Met Abandons Blackface, a Look at the Legacy of African-Americans in Opera," *Hyperallergic. com.* August 3, 2015, www.hyperallergic.com/226687/as-the-met-abandons-blackface-a-look-at-the-legacy-of-african-americans-in-opera/

Edward Rothstein, "Black Composers" Striving for More," *New York Times*, April 14, 1994, www.nytimes. com/1994/04/14/arts/black-composers-of-classical-music-striving-for-more.html?pagewanted=2

William Robin, "Great Divide at the Concert Hall," *New York Times*, August 10, 2014, www.nytimes.com/2014/08/10/ arts/music/black-composers-discuss-the-role-of-race.html?_ r=0

Mallika Rao, "Black Classical Musicians: A Case Study In Beating The Odds," *Huffington Post*, April 30, 2013, www. huffingtonpost.com/2013/04/30/african-americans-in-classical-music_n_3188436.html

Q& A: Aaron P. Dworkin, *The Guardian*, May 10, 2013, www.theguardian.com/music/2013/may/10/rps-international-honorary-membership-aaron-p-dworkin-sphinx-organization

Alison Kinney, "As the Met Abandons Blackface, a Look

at the Legacy of African-Americans in Opera," *hyperallergic. com*, August 3, 2015, www.hyperallergic. com/226687/as-the-met-abandons-blackface-a-look-at-the-legacy-of-african-americans-in-opera/

CHAPTER 5: INVISIBLE PEOPLE?

www.en.wikipedia.org/wiki/Bach_to_the_Blues

www.30sjazz.com/videos/art-tatum-1/humoresque. html

www.en.wikipedia.org/wiki/Waltz_for_Debby_(1962_album)

www.en.wikipedia.org/wiki/Gunther_Schuller

"Duke Ellington: The Composer, Pt 1," NPR, November 19, 2008, www.npr.org/2008/11/19/97193567/duke-ellington-the-composer-pt-1

www.en.wikipedia.org/wiki/Duke_Ellington%27s_Sacred_Concerts

www.jass.com/wcook.html

"Rhythms in Classical Music," *Talk Classical*, April 10, 2010, www.talkclassical.com/8844-rhythms-used-classical-music.html

"Baroque and Jazz Compared," *Syncrat*, January 7, 2005, www.syncrat.com/posts/5301/baroque-early-jazz-compared

Tal Livingston, "Classical Vs. Jazz: Crossing the Great Divide," *I Care if You Listen*, October 3, 2011, www.icareifyoulisten.com/2011/10/classical-vs-jazz-crossing-the-great-divide/

Paul Hoffman, "The Inherent Compatibility of Jazz and

Classical Music," nd

www.mhrrecords.com/articlesandessays/essay01.html

www.en.wikipedia.org/wiki/Epitaph_(Charles_Mingus_album)

Ethan Iverson, "Keith Jarrett Goes Classical," *Downbeat*, October 2013, www.downbeat.com/microsites/ecm-jarrett/post_1-Jarrett-goes-classical.html

www.en.wikipedia.org/wiki/Chick_Corea

Nick Morrison, "From Bach To Satie: Jazz Takes On Classical," NPR, May 10, 2011, www.npr.org/sections/ablogsupreme/2011/05/13/136137614/from-bach-to-satie-jazz-takes-on-classical

Billy Taylor, "Jazz, America's Classical Music." nd., www.billytaylorjazz.com/Jazz.pdf

# Bibliography

Raoul Abdul, *Blacks in Classical Music,* *(New York: Dodd-Mead, 1978).*

Gabriel Banat, *The Chevalier de Saint-Georges: Virtuoso of the Sword and the Bow* (London: Pendragon Press, 2006).

Andras Batta, *Opera: Composers, Works, Performers* (Rome: H.F. Ullmann Publishing, 2009).

William Berger, *Verdi With a Vengeance: An Energetic Guide to the Life and Complete Works of the King of Opera* (New York: Vintage Press, 2000).

George J. Beulow, *A History of Baroque Music* (Bloomington, In.: Indiana University Press, 2004).

Christopher A. Brooks, *Roland Hayes: The Legacy of an American Tenor* (Bloomington, In.: Indiana University Press, 2014).

Harry T. Burleigh, The Spirituals of Harry T. Burleigh (Songbook), (Van Nuys, Ca.: Alfred Music, 1985).

James H. Cone, *The Spirituals and the Blues: An Interpretation* (New York: Orbis Books, 1992).

John Gray, *Blacks in Classical Music: A Bibliographical Guide to Composers, Performers, and Ensembles (Music Reference Collection)* (New York: Greenwood Books, 1988).

Jeffrey Green, *Samuel Coleridge-Taylor, a Musical Life* (New York: Routledge, 2011).

William Hyland, *George Gershwin: A New Biography* (New York: Praeger, 2003).

Earl Ofari Hutchinson, *Beethoven and Me: A Beginner's Guide to Classical Music* (Los Angeles: Middle Passage Press, 2015).

Adam Keiler, *Marian Anderson: A Singer's Journey: The First Comprehensive Biography* (New York: Scribner, 2000)

Arbie Orenstein, *Ravel: Man and Musician* (New York: Dover Books, 2011).

Bernard L. Peterson Jr., *Profiles of African-American Stage Performers and Theatre People*, 1816-1960 (New York; Greenwood Press, 2000).

Clifford D. Panton, Jr. *George Augustus Polgreen Bridgetower: Violin Virtuoso and Composer of Color in Late 18th Century Europe* (Lewiston, N.Y.: Edwin Mellen Press, 2005).

Howard Pollack, *Aaron Copland: The Life and Work of an Uncommon Man (Music in American Life)* (Champagne, Ill: University of Illinois Press, 2000).

Paul Robeson Jr., *The Undiscovered Paul Robeson, An Artist's Journey, 1898-1939* (New York: Wiley, 2001).

Charles Rosen, *The Classical Style: Haydn, Mozart, Beethoven (Expanded Edition)* (New York: W.W. Norton, 1988).

Ross Russell, *Bird Lives!: The High Life And Hard Times Of Charlie (yardbird) Parker* (New York: DaCapo Press, 1996).

Grover Sales, *Jazz: America's Classical Music* (New York: DaCapo Press, 1992).

Ignatius Sancho, *Letters of the Late Ignatius Sancho, an African* (London: Cosimo Classics, 2005).

Walter E. Smith, *The Black Mozart: Le Chevalier de Saint-Georges*, (New York: Authorhouse, 2004).

Frederic Spotts, *Bayreuth: A History of the Wagner Festival* (New Haven: Yale University Press, 1996).

Terry Teachout, *Duke: A Life of Duke Ellington* (New York: Avery, 2013).

Billy Taylor, *Jazz Piano: A Jazz History* (New York: William C. Brown Co, 1982).

Giuseppi Verdi, *Aïda Paperback* (Charleston, S.C.: Nabu Press, 2011).

Robert Lee Watt, *The Black Horn: The Story of Classical French Hornist Robert Lee Watt (African-American Cultural Theory and Heritage)* (New York: Rowman & Littlefield Publishers, 2014).

Eric Walter White, *Stravinsky: The Composer and His Works* (Berkeley: University of California Press, 1985).

Christoph Wolff, *Johann Sebastian Bach: The Learned Musician* (New York: W.W. Norton, 2001).

# *Index*

# About the Author

Earl Ofari Hutchinson has an M.A. in Humanities from California State University, Dominguez Hills that included the Humanities course series on the advanced study of music, focusing on concepts of meaning and form in music. He is a sustaining member of the American Musicological Society. He has for a decade programed, featured and promoted classical music on the KPFK-Pacifica Radio Network.

From1995 to 2015, he attended nearly 500 concerts by nearly every nationally and internationally known major orchestra, and that featured many of the top virtuoso performers, and attended many major festivals including the Aspen, Bach Carmel, and the Ojai Festival. He has interviewed many of the leading classical conductors, composers, and performers, He has written about classical musical developments in his columns. He moderated the prestigious panel of classical artists and musicologists on the works of Dimitri Shostakovich. He has attended and participated in numerous concert lectures and preconcert lectures. He completed the Comprehensive Music Study Series based on The History of Western Music at West Los Angeles College and studied music theory and history at the Pasadena Conservatory of Music.